A FIELD FOR EXPLOITS
Training L
The Salvai

General Eva Bı
Major Stephen Court

*The Salvation Army leader training system
'offers to the enterprise and daring of our best youth
a field for exploits'.*
General Bramwell Booth

Salvation Books
The Salvation Army International Headquarters
London, United Kingdom

Copyright © 2012
The General of The Salvation Army

ISBN 978-0-85412-843-3

Cover design by Jooles Tostevin
Project editors: Major David Dalziel and Paul Mortlock

Unless stated otherwise, Scripture references
have been updated from the original text and are taken from
the Holy Bible, New International Version,
Copyright © 1979, 1984, 2011 by Biblica,
formerly International Bible Society
Revised and updated 2011 by Hodder & Stoughton

Other Scripture references from:
ASV: American Standard Version
ESV: English Standard Version
JBP: J.B. Phillips
KJV: King James Version
NASB: New American Standard Bible
NEB: New English Bible
NIV 1984: New International Version 1984
RSV: Revised Standard Version

Published by Salvation Books
The Salvation Army International Headquarters
101 Queen Victoria Street, London EC4V 4EH, United Kingdom

Printed in the UK by CPI Group (UK) Ltd, Croydon, CR0 4YY

A FIELD FOR EXPLOITS
Training Leaders for
The Salvation Army

Contents

		Page No
Acknowledgements		vi
Introduction – Major Stephen Court		vii
Chapter 1	*The Aim of Leader Training* General Bramwell Booth	1
Chapter 2	*The Message and the Messenger* General Bramwell Booth	13
Chapter 3	*Salvationism* Mrs General Florence Booth	29
Chapter 4	*The Ethos of Leader Training* Mrs General Florence Booth	45
Chapter 5	*We Believe in Miracles:* *Development of Character* Lieut-Colonel Catherine Bramwell-Booth	57
Chapter 6	*Training Character* General Albert Orsborn	73
Chapter 7	*Profile of Leadership – the Training Principal,* *Today and Tomorrow* General Erik Wickberg	83
Chapter 8	*Training Evangelists* General Erik Wickberg	95
Chapter 9	*Men and Women Like Us: the Aims and* *Philosophy of Salvation Army Leader Training* Commissioner Arnold Brown	109
Chapter 10	*Contextualisation and Other Dynamics* *of the Smaller Training System* Major Paul Rader	117

Chapter 11	***Our Future and* The *Future***	141
	Commissioner Arnold Brown	
Chapter 12	***A Theology of Officership***	155
	Colonel Eva Burrows	
Chapter 13	***Cross-cultural Training***	171
	Captain Clive Adams	
Chapter 14	***Spiritual Leadership in The Salvation Army***	177
	Dr Jonathan S. Raymond	
Chapter 15	***Head, Hands and Heart – The Training of Salvation Army Officers (Leaders)***	191
	General Eva Burrows (Retired)	
Chapter 16	***By Many Prayers and Tears – Spiritual Leadership in The Salvation Army***	195
	General Eva Burrows (Retired)	
Chapter 17	***21st Century Leadership***	207
	General Eva Burrows (Retired)	
Chapter 18	***Conclusion – 'Ten to Take Away'***	217
	Major Stephen Court	

Potted Biographies of Authors	219

Acknowledgements

WITHOUT William and Catherine Booth, the founding leaders of The Salvation Army, there would be no book. Without the original contributors to the four International Training Councils, there would be no book. Without the continuing heroics of thousands of leaders in thousands of towns and cities around the world, there would be no book.

And without the participation of Margaret Coombridge, Louise Robinson, Commissioner Wesley Harris and Sonia D'Silva, who worked with the manuscripts, there would be no book. Without the editing work of Major David Dalziel, Paul Mortlock and Lieut-Colonel Laurie Robertson at International Headquarters, there would be no book.

The shortcomings are ours. The strengths belong to the whole Salvation Army.

General Eva Burrows (Retired)
Major Stephen Court
September 2012

Introduction

THE Salvation Army, this revolutionary movement of covenanted warriors exercising holy passion to win the world for Jesus, has produced heroic leaders on every continent. These larger-than-life personalities have transformed the lives of countless hurting people and their families and descendants as well as systems and practices and cultures.

But what is more amazing about leader training in The Salvation Army is what it produces from humble beginnings. Our Generals could look at our local officers and officers and quote the apostle Paul with some authority when he said, 'Not many of you were wise by human standards; not many were influential; not many were of noble birth' (1 Corinthians 1:26).

And yet many of these Salvation Army leaders shocked communities by the power and authority of their leadership. The *un*wise and *un*influential and *ig*noble (by Paul's standards above) led significant groups of people, organised massive initiatives, managed seven-digit budgets – and we're just talking about the local-level leadership! At senior levels you think in terms of tens of thousands of people and national level issues and then add a few zeros to the budgets.

How does The Salvation Army do it? It isn't about fame. Salvation Army leaders aren't in it to get their names in lights. To prove it, try to list the last five territorial commanders in the country where you live. Even the most devoted Salvationists might have a difficult time with that one.

What is it? As Christian readers might expect, some of this can be explained by the Holy Spirit's empowerment of the lives of devoted servants, and Salvation Army leaders from the General to local officers fit that description. But a substantial component of the success can be found in the Army's leader training system.

That said, you might expect there to be a stack of Salvation Army leadership books on the market. In fact there are only a few. They are helpful and we recommend them, but the leadership training principles of The Salvation Army have not been published for the benefit of readers around the world. Until now.

A Field for Exploits is intended to fill this gap and provide an understanding of the motivations and purposes of Salvation Army leader training. This book is not just the thoughts of a handful of people however, even though one of them – General Eva Burrows – was one of our movement's outstanding world leaders from 1986 to 1993. It is more than that.

Four times in its history, The Salvation Army has organised International Training Councils – 1925, 1951, 1974 and 2001. These fairly-evenly-spaced events gathered the best leader-trainers from around the world to discuss best practice for training leaders in this unique movement and to learn from it. After each event, the presented papers were collected for limited dissemination. These represent the very best Salvation Army perspectives on training leaders for each period. Some of the lectures were representative of their day. Others stand out beyond their era and offer to us lessons relevant to the 21st century.

We have collected some of these papers – by Generals Bramwell Booth, Albert Orsborn, Erik Wickberg, Arnold Brown, Paul A. Rader and Eva Burrows, as well as by other influential leaders at the various councils (keeping their ranks at the time of writing). To broaden the application for readers and to increase accessibility, we have edited, where it makes sense, so that it is not limited to Salvation Army officership training. So, there have been some reductions in length and throughout the majority of the book we have changed 'officer' to 'leader', 'cadet' to 'learner', and 'training college/garrison' to 'training system' or simply 'training'. The main text of the book reflects current editorial style, but the footnote references taken from the original publications retain their use of capitalisation, terminology, and so on.

Our choice of 'learner' to replace cadet should be understood as something more practical than 'student', more formal than 'apprentice', more mainstream than 'disciple', and more rigorous than 'trainee'. Though originally addressing officers and cadets, the lessons apply to leaders and learners of all kinds throughout The Salvation Army. The purposes and intentions of the original writers have not been changed in any way. Where single words or short phrases have been updated, footnotes should enable the reader to quote the original text. Similarly, where longer sentences or paragraphs have been abridged, this too is indicated by footnotes. However, it is impossible to indicate every instance where a section of text has simply been omitted.

Each updated chapter is accompanied by a reading guide and discussion starters intended to stimulate debate surrounding issues of adapting and adopting the lessons on your local front.

Also, General Burrows contributes other chapters containing lessons gleaned from her experience as global leader of The Salvation Army.

The entire package offers insight into the combined wisdom of The Salvation Army on leadership training over many decades. On their best days Salvation Army training systems provide for the daring and enterprise of our best youth 'a field for exploits'. May these pages open up a wide expanse and provide deep inspiration so you will attempt, experiment, explore and risk in your leader training and in your salvation warfare.

Major Stephen Court
September 2012

Chapter 1
The Aim of Leader Training[1]
by General Bramwell Booth
International Training Staff Council 1925

IN the opening paragraph of *Orders and Regulations (O&R) for the Training of Officers*, the object of training is stated as follows:
> The supreme object to be kept in view in the training work shall be the production of Blood-and-Fire officers; that is, officers possessing the Spirit, and able to sustain and advance the interests of The Salvation Army, in all its departments and in all its spheres of operation.

This very broad statement sets out our chief aim. The chief aim involves subordinate aims, for there are lesser objectives which harmonise with the greater objective, and which bring certain considerations and advantages into view. Of such advantages I will mention three.

1. Reinforcement for the field

In the first place, the training of new leaders enables us to send forth year by year a new stream of holy influence, zeal and love into the field, amongst the leaders already serving. That is one of the most important of the minor advantages – minor only in relation to the supreme object – which our leader training system affords. I am sure you must all have realised again and again what a tremendous power it is in any section of Army work to have the constant accretion, year by year, of this new life, this earnest zeal, this fresh spirit of love for God and for souls. It challenges us. It reminds us of the standard which may have been allowed to droop.[2]

I constantly hear of the advantages in the way of blessing, joy and inspiration which the young leaders, fresh from leader training, bring to older leaders in the field. Tragically those younger leaders are often more or less sacrificed[3] to the conservatism of some of the older leaders who

1

have become – I will not say backsliders – slow and set in their ways. In spite of this, however, the young leader, even though he fails to move his senior, may have quite a considerable influence on the corps, on the soldiers, and on possible candidates for leadership.

But one of my hopes is that, increasingly, these new people, with their fresh zeal,[4] may be the means of rekindling in older leaders the ideals and aspirations which once were theirs, and which have diminished a little under the weariness of the war. I scarcely go anywhere without finding evidence of the influence of our training systems in the field itself, or without hearing of younger leaders who are helping older leaders[5] who may have lost ground to recover former love and enthusiasm.

2. An open door

Another of those allied aims which come into view with the main objective is *the open door*, the awaiting opportunity, which leader training affords. To some young man may be made the remark, 'You ought to give yourself to God.' He is moved and agrees. The other goes on, 'You ought to devote yourself to service for mankind.' Again 'Yes.' 'You ought to be fully consecrated to God in the life you now live.' He agrees. But because he cannot see a definite way of obedience before him, no lasting impression is made. The moment of great impulse passes by. To reverse the familiar idiom [*hitch your wagon to a star*], there is a star, but no wagon.

How different it is when the Salvation Army officer says to such a young man, 'God is calling you. There is an open door before you. You ought to go into training.'[6] This presentation of a tangible opportunity grips him. The vision of that open door is not easily blotted out.

Many promising young men and women[7] who desire to serve God and bless their generation are held back because they feel unequal to the challenge. They can be pointed to leader training and what it is able to accomplish for and through them. Now, remember, the better we train our leaders, the better the candidates we attract.[8]

I hope the day will come when we shall be able to train our soldiers as local officers, that there will be in every land a great institution where each soldier who is going to take up a local officer commission, at any rate on a census board [pastoral care council], must come and spend a month, or two or three months, to be trained for the work. I may not live to see that day, but I am quite sure it will come.

Recently I had 40 bandmasters for 10 days' training in the staff institute here. Those 40 men, who have under them 1,100 bandsmen, are in themselves an outstanding manifestation of Salvation Army ability and zeal. The influence and instruction of those 10 days is issuing powerfully in the corps they represent.[9]

3. Opportunity for adventure

[10]A third advantage which I see in leader training is that it offers to the enterprise and daring of our best youth *a field for exploits*. New outlets for love and energy have constantly been discovered and new strategies deployed that have influenced the whole Army. For example, the Cellar, Gutter and Garret Brigade, which afterwards became the Slum Work and has since reached across the world, started at the first training garrison.

The Slum Work was found to be so successful it became a normal component of the field operations. We invited some soldiers to help us. They were able to do slum work only by living in the slums, so we put them down to live amongst the people who needed their help. That was how we reached the idea of living amongst the slum people. That was how we went incarnational!

In different parts of the world other strategies have emerged, because[11] the youth of the Army, the learners in leader training, have had imagination, vision, and enterprise, and have also had the opportunity to follow the promptings of their hearts.

I think you ought to be very liberal in watching over your learners. The normal must not be unalterable.[12] If a learner is 'enthused' about any particular work – is, for example, moved to raid the drinking saloons, or to shout the claims of God in the cinemas or in the theatres between the acts, or to break out in some other 'disorderly' way in the right spirit – do not 'sit' on him. Say, rather, 'I would like to hear about this. Have you prayed about it? Take Smith with you next time, and see if you can infect him and then report to me again.'

With a little wise encouragement, your leader training system may become the frequent birthplace of new things. Your learners will strike on things that nobody else has thought of. This relationship should be[13] a hot-house of new plants – plants which at first may be delicate, but with attention and encouragement may become sturdy trees whose leaves will be for the healing of the nations.

The spiritual life of the learner

But I must come closer, and deal with one or two aims of training in regard to the spiritual life and religious experience of your learners. In the first place, you are responsible for their integrity. I am thinking of 'integrity' in the strictest sense of the term. We must ourselves search our learners on integrity, and teach them to search themselves. No amount of enthusiasm or sacrifice will take the place of integrity,[14] any more than glorious stonework on a building will compensate for a faulty plan or a shifty foundation.

Many learners are willing to make great sacrifices for God and the Army, and yet they fail in some perfectly simple matter of integrity in their own lives and experience. For starters,[15] there is the question of clearing up old darkness, failure, mistake, sin. These things belong to the past, but they seriously affect the present, if they have never been fully brought into the light.

I know what I am talking about when I beg you to deal more fervently and courageously with learners about their past. No matter what they feel or say, or what sacrifices they make, if some rotten place is left in the foundation, the structure is bound to fall, and will probably crush them when it falls, besides doing serious hurt to the Kingdom of God.

Save yourself much time and trouble in the future by efficiently searching your learners on integrity in your first meetings and early days of training. Often, after three[16] months of a session a learner brings something to light that makes you say, 'If only we had known this at the beginning!' Or, at the end of six months some shadow from the past emerges, that suddenly explains the wobbling weakness, which would not have arisen had the matter been faced boldly at first. Find better ways to expose them to these issues and confront them with these sins or hurts quickly. Unsolved problems, unfaced difficulties, will drag on the wheels more and more as the war advances.[17]

I am surprised, globally, that those with smaller groups of learners often fail in this respect. The smaller systems – which, of course, are in the majority – train, in the aggregate, more leaders than the larger. Always remember, you who are working in the smaller systems, that you belong to the fraternity which does the bulk of the training. The breakages which come from this and other causes are relatively greater in the smaller groups, although in those groups there is usually more time and strength to devote to each individual, and we have a right to expect that the fruit there will be more permanent and satisfactory.[18]

Effective dealing with potential learners[19]

This points to another great need – to deal more effectively with potential learners. To improve our learner recruitment, we must improve the leader. A potential learner begins the leader training process, and when he has been involved a month, out comes some confession of inward backsliding or worldliness. Why didn't the leader find this out? If you asked me to answer this question I'd reply with another: why didn't you make the kind of leader who would have found it all out?

It is absolutely essential to all else that you do, that you should yourself first make sure of the integrity[20] of the learner. The confessions at the mercy seat are desirable and beautiful, but you must look beyond those for the evidence of integrity in the lives of your learners. No matter what they say, look for obvious signs of integrity. I am confident that you are with me in this matter, and that you would rather raise up six leaders who will endure to the end than 600 who will weaken and break down.

While evil, especially hidden evil, remains in the heart of your learners, you will never be able to teach them to live lives pleasing to God. Learners[21] should make true submission to God – surrender their wills – when they seek for and claim full salvation. Holiness is a matter of the will. It is, especially in its reflective character, a condition of cleansing by the precious blood, but as a part of daily life and experience it depends upon the submitted will. It is essential that our learners and leaders should be submitted in this manner.[22] The Bible says a great deal about being servants of God, but the word which has been translated 'servant' might more correctly have been translated 'slave'. The underlying idea in all such references to servants is the idea of being mastered, that God's people are not their own, that they are under the will of another, that they are mastered, and that they have submitted wholly to the claims of their Master.

Some of us have been brought to submission by his providence; some by his afflictions, those which he bore himself and those which he laid upon us; some by the attractions of his wonderful love. But, by whatever means, the great fact is that we have been bowed down. We have said, 'Not my will, but yours, be done.' I don't need to say[23] that we shall do little with our learners unless we ourselves come to the point of complete submission to God, and are able to teach that submission to them. I know that this training in submission is difficult, if only because we have so many different characters to deal with, each presenting its individual problem, and also because we have to encompass it in so short a time. I wonder how far you feel that the term of leader training ought to be extended. How much would it advantage the learner? Of course, a question of cost is involved, but I prophesy that money is not going to be so great a difficulty for you in the future as in the past.

Submission to the will of God

A wise man has said that the whole of religion is submission to the will of God. Whether or not we agree, there certainly can be no true Christianity without submission. Try to influence your learners to see this essential truth.[24] Bring them to the point at which they can say, 'Whatever comes, I will take it from him.'

Sin was born on this earth when man positioned his will against God's will. In that moment, he fell and became a creature of sin, the dupe of the tempter. Sin in the world today arises from the stubborn resistance of people's will to God's. Unless we can bring our learners in their youth to see that submission to God is necessary to safely build their relationship with God,²⁵ they will never accomplish what we want them to accomplish.

In reading the lives of the saints of God of the past – our own dear saints, for our saints are a match for any other saints! – do you not always find that there came a time in life, perhaps early, perhaps later, when the song of submission arose in the heart? I want that song to break forth from our youngest leaders before they have been broken by affliction or shaken by overwhelming sorrow.

Affliction and sorrow, trial and bereavement are the means by which many people, who would not otherwise learn submission, are brought to surrender their wills to God. But we aim to bring our learners to that blessed union with God, that state of complete submission, while they are training with us. This is the only way they can be saved from lost hours, wasted opportunities and futile regrets.²⁶

We aim to show them that, by the power of the Holy Ghost, they can enter immediately into that state of submission which uninstructed and wilful souls only attain, if at all, after years of affliction. There is no virtue in bereavement or affliction, nothing even in the presence of death – either for ourselves or those we love – that has any essential significance in the development of the soul. But those things are means that God often uses to bring the soul to submission.

So I ask you to exert every power you can to bring your learners to that state of submission – that spirit which says, 'Never mind me, don't bother about me; let it be God's will, the Army's will.' Then they will become effective, because, instead of wanting to pick and choose, and growing rebellious in the first success they attain, and talking about their rights, they will be ready to do what God and the Army require. Train them in submission.

Tests for reality

Some tests must be introduced in the leader training in order to prove how far the submissiveness of your learners is real. I was talking to a young leader who told me that there was one blessing he had while training which he could never forget.

'I was always a person,' he said, 'who thought something of myself.'

'I am not sure,' I put in, 'that that is not one of your difficulties now.'

'No,' he said, 'I am saved from it, and it came about in a strange way. I liked to have my own way, and I was not inclined to the pace and demands[27] of training. One day I was told to fall in outside with nine other cadets and wait for a certain officer. It was raining. We waited for 20 minutes, and were wet through before the order was cancelled. Then I had to go in and change, as did the others. I had been feeling anything but submissive, but I went into my bedroom, got on my knees, and fought that battle out once and for all. I said, "Very well, if that is what you want of me, I am ready to give up my own way and my own preferences." I have never had any more trouble with myself.'

That was an extreme case, and probably came about through an oversight, but if there was no other way of getting hold of that man, it's a good thing they got soaked.[28]

Lowliness of mind

Associated with submission is humility; not quite the same thing, for submission has more to do with action – with deeds and events – whereas humility is a state of mind. The humble man looks out upon life from a lowly point of view:

He that is down need fear no fall,
He that is low no pride.

(Louisa May Alcott)

Some young people show an arrogant spirit which needs correction. Humility means a low estimate of oneself, which in turn leads to a warm appreciation of the gifts and qualities of others. Superiority makes it impossible to notice the goodness and distinctiveness of those around us. By calling ourselves big, we make everyone little.[29]

Solomon said, 'The fear of the Lord is the beginning of wisdom' (Proverbs 9:10). That implies submission before God, looking up to him in his wisdom with a lowly heart and mind. The apostle spoke of the importance of serving 'the Lord with great humility and with tears' (Acts 20:19). He associated with humility the tenderness of which tears are often the token. Arrogance and conceit are seldom tender.[30] They grow harder until nothing moves them.

I know that here I am asking much. Some of you are dealing with cold, self-centred, democratic people, self-confident, acknowledging but few loyalties. It is difficult to convince them that they should be submissive and humble. But the standards which God has set up cannot be changed because we find that the times have changed. It is still one of the conditions upon which his blessings are given that there shall be submissiveness, humility, tenderness. I know how essential this is. I have been observing people, and God's ways with people, for close to 60 years, and I say to you in all seriousness that it is the humble in spirit whom God delights to honour. When from his heart, without a big show, a man says, 'O God, I come and submit to you,' then God says, 'Very well, I will use you.'[31] That is what we want with our learners.

Reading Guide

Sometimes prejudice against anything old taints our reading of early Salvation Army texts. We dismiss the passion as a cultural relic. And the heroic sacrifice that oozes from the pages is like a foreign language that we cannot comprehend. And so we write it off, or at best consider it as a history piece.

But General Bramwell Booth was speaking in 1925, near the end of his earthly life, of the accumulated wisdom of Salvation Army training from experience in many countries, in many challenging circumstances, and in the heat of revival, over the previous 50 years. It is to our poverty that we dismiss the teachings as irrelevant.

While the language can be flowery at times, the sentiment expressed is unvarnished and sincere. It is refreshing to read the heart of a proven warrior sharing on leadership. That's why we've included it here.

The big takeaway is *a field for exploits*. Bramwell Booth is describing the training systems of that day as providing for the daring and enterprise of our best soldiers, *a field for exploits*. This is a stage on which great soldiers accomplish great feats above and beyond the call of duty. So, part of this system is intended to provide space for experimenting and

A Field for Exploits

exploring and initiating. There is meant to be teaching and training and discipling, yes. But there is also a culture nurtured that enables and empowers leaders and budding leaders to innovate and take risks.

Training systems today will inevitably look significantly different from that upon which Bramwell Booth based his teaching here. However, we will do well if we can create an environment in which our learners are challenged and stimulated and spurred on to both love and good deeds – and to great exploits of their own.

Discussion Starters

1. On pages 2-3, Bramwell Booth anticipates the day when soldiers go off for a month of special training to become local officers. That day hasn't yet arrived. Do you think its time has come? How might it look? What should be taught?

2. There is a strong case made to develop within learners a state of submission to the will of God. This runs contrary to popular culture today. Is Booth at odds only with popular culture or also with popular Christianity? Should submission be emphasised more within Christianity? If so, how?

3. In the section 'Tests for Reality' on pages 7-8, Bramwell Booth tells the story of a 20-minute rain shower that changed a life. What reality tests have you experienced? How have they changed things for you?

---

[1] *Training Staff Council Lectures 1925*, 'The Aim of Training – I', 19, International Headquarters (IHQ), 1925.
[2] It comes into the fields of our ordinary activity as a challenge. It recalls us to the standard which may have been allowed to droop.
[3] inspiration which the young Officers, fresh from the Training Garrison, bring to older officers in the Field. Alas! those younger Officers are often more or less sacrificed…
[4] But one of my hopes is that, more and more, these new people, with their morning freshness, may be the means…
[5] …the influence of one or other of the Training Garrisons in the Field itself, or without hearing of Lieutenants and Captains who are helping older Officers…
[6] …to the Training Garrison.
[7] …fellows, are held back because they feel themselves unequal to the task. They can be pointed to the Training Garrison…

8. And in that connexion I want it to be remembered that the better we do the Training Work, the more promising will be the Candidates whom we shall attract.
9. The influences that were brought to bear upon them, and the instruction that was given them, during those ten days are now reissuing powerfully in the Corps they represent.
10. *The following two paragraphs are heavily abridged, and Major Court then sums them up by writing 'That was how we went incarnational!'*
11. Other avenues of work have opened to us in different parts of the world, because…
12. The normal routine in the Training Garrison must not…
13. The Training Garrison should be…
14. In the first place, I want to say that you are responsible for his rectitude – his 'rightness'. I am thinking of 'rightness' in the strictest sense of the term. We must ourselves search the Cadet as to his rightness, and teach him to search himself. No amount of enthusiasm or sacrifice will take the place of rightness…
15. To begin with…
16. In the first interviews and the early days of Training a more efficient searching of the Cadets as to their rightness would probably save a great deal of time and labour afterwards. Often after three…
17. …and you find the sudden explanation of the wobbling, of the weakness, which would not have arisen had the matter been faced out boldly at the first. It is open to you all to find some better method of bringing the Cadets more quickly face to face with these things. Unsolved problems, unfaced difficulties will drag on the wheels more and more as the journey goes on.
18. I am surprised, when I look into the reports from the different countries, to find that you of the smaller Training Garrisons often fail in this respect. The smaller Garrisons – which, of course, are in the majority – train, in the aggregate, more Officers than the larger. Always remember, you who are working in the smaller Garrisons, that you belong to the fraternity which does the bulk of the Training! The breakages which come from this and other causes are relatively greater in the lesser Garrisons, although, in those Garrisons, there is usually more time and strength to devote to each individual, and we have a right to expect that the fruit there will be more permanent and satisfactory. *[Bramwell Booth's words here are particularly interesting in relation to Major Paul Rader's contribution from 1974.]*
19. *Potential learners = Candidates. The following paragraph is heavily abridged.*
20. *'Integrity' replaces 'rightness' in the original, as above.*
21. Those Cadets who are intelligently instructed…
22. It is specially important that our Cadets and Officers should be in this state of submission.
23. 'Not my will, but Thine, be done.' Need I say…
24. …great necessity.
25. Unless we can bring these Cadets in their youth to see that submission to God is a necessary condition if they are to build with safety their personal religion,…
26. But we seek to bring our Cadets to that blessed union with God, and that state of complete submission while they are with us in the Training Garrisons. Thus only will they be…
27. hurry and bustle…
28. it was well it occurred.
29. If we assume an attitude of superiority we shall fail to notice the goodness and distinctiveness of those around us. Calling ourselves big, we shall call all else little.
30. The arrogant and conceited are seldom able to be tender.
31. 'Very well, I will make use of you.'

Chapter 2
The Message and the Messenger[32]
by General Bramwell Booth
International Training Staff Council 1925

WE are a people supremely interested in and devoted to the salvation of people. That is our great idea. We have what some people consider an unhealthy passion for the salvation of our generation.[33]

In the Bible, God has employed many figures to describe, as he has determined many means to accomplish, the great end of people's salvation. We find there that God's relations with people in the matter of their salvation are described in various ways.[34] We have the idea of a holy warfare between good and evil, and the idea of a great emancipation from bondage or slavery. Much of the language of the Bible – in both the Old and New Testaments – indicates also a great effort to deliver people from condemnation, and to cancel the penalties of their sin.

Much of the Bible is not easily understood, but it will become clearer if it is viewed through the salvation lens[35] – that in some way a great effort is being made, a great scheme of redemption is being worked out, a great plan of new life is in progress so that people may be set free from their sin and from the condemnation which results from it.

Perhaps the most striking of all these ideas, is that introducing people to God *will be the remedy for their ills.*[36] If people are made to know God, from whom they have been estranged – if their little apprehensions are opened to some kind of conception of what he is – then the machinery is put in motion for remedying the awful ills from which they suffer. One of the great promises of the Old Testament is: 'I will give them a heart to know…I am the Lord' (Jeremiah 24:7).

The New Testament has nothing plainer and simpler than the prayer of the Apostle, that we may 'know this love that surpasses knowledge –

that you may be filled to the measure of all the fullness of God' (Ephesians 3:19). 'Now this is eternal life: that they know you, the only true God, and Jesus Christ, whom you have sent' (John 17:3). Hallelujah![37]

And, again, there is that majestic figure – conveying perhaps the most wonderful of all the promises relating to the future triumph of good – that 'the earth will be filled with the knowledge of the glory of the Lord as the waters cover the sea' (Habakkuk 2:14).

The charge to the Army

Now, in thinking of many aspects of the Army, I have been impressed by the thought that our primary and greatest responsibility is to make God known. It is our role and calling to see to the fulfilment of some, at any rate, of these promises and directions. It is our special burden to extend this experience to all people knowing, not only a Divine Father, but a sufficient Saviour. So our great purpose is to spread the knowledge of God. We have been raised up, equipped, deployed and sustained until this day by the power of the Holy Spirit to spread among people the experience of knowing (not knowing about) our Holy God and of Jesus Christ whom he has sent.[38]

I fully realise that there are many incidental activities. Every big stream has many tributaries, and often is itself a feeder of other streams, although its main business is to flow on to the sea. So with us, this spreading of the knowledge of God, this proclamation of his Son, has come to have associated with it various enterprises, which at first glance may not seem directly concerned with the main mission. Close examination, however, reveals that every department[39] is intended to assist this great business of spreading the light of God, making people know their Father, opening their hearts to recognise Jesus Christ as their Saviour.

All our comrades everywhere, join in this. What a grand company our leaders constitute! Do you not feel it? Does not something arise in your heart with regard to them, similar to the feelings you have for your own family, or for those you specially love? Does not your heart go out especially to those of them who are fighting on the very borders of the world's civilisation, or are holding up their little light in some dark and crowded city? Does not the thought of them make your heart glow? And I say to you that all this great company, spread over so many lands, engaged in operations so diverse, are striving for this great end – getting everyone to know God personally.[40]

A message from God

Now, thinking of the Army in this way, it seems to me that one thing is clear. We have a message from God. We have something to communicate. We have received a message from God for the world. We can go farther, and say that the message is for the whole world. No doubt we may regard ourselves as specially called to the most faulty, the most degraded, the most needy. We quote with joy and pride our dear old General's words: 'Go for souls, and go for the worst!' But while it is true that we do go for certain special sections and classes, whose extremity appears to us most dire, and in the approach to whom we have acquired a special skill, yet the message we have received of God to give to the people is a message for all sections and all classes, for all the people. It is a message, which will be found to fit the human heart in all circumstances, of all races and nations, in all social degrees, at all intellectual levels.

We may fittingly compare this message with light. It is a message of illumination, for it is a message of condemnation, of the revelation of sin, of salvation from sin. Then it is a message of reconciliation with God. Our message is one that awakens the conscience, revealing the depth to which a person has fallen and the height to which one may attain, showing on the one hand the condemnation that sin brings, and on the other the means of salvation from sin's power and penalty.

A message peculiar to us

I think that our message is peculiar to us in some ways. Some may be inclined to say, 'Haven't similar messages been preached in the past?' The answer is 'Yes' and 'No.' There have, no doubt, been some messages similar in fundamentals to our own. But our message seems to me to have in it one element of vital importance which makes it stand out a little from the others.

The apostles received their message from the human lips of their Divine Master. They took it direct from him. Even the critics, even those who doubt the authenticity of the records, admit that whatever teaching the apostles did receive to set forth, they received from the lips of Jesus Christ.[41]

Though they may not have been successful in comprehending it all in its fullest meaning, or in recording it all in its fullest details, they did make effective use of it in their own day. The fruits which came of it were wonderfully like the fruits which have come from the declaration of our message in our day. If I had time I could show you many startling similarities, both in the message itself and in its results.

Those who followed the apostles during the first two or three hundred years after Christ no doubt had a message which was received from the heart of God through the Holy Spirit. That message sustained them in their particular circumstances. It carried them through the most dreadful conflicts. It kept alive the little flame of witness in that seat of iniquity which is sometimes called the Roman Empire. That message fitted their specific condition and circumstance, and it emphasised the maintenance of the life which God had planted within them,[42] and the preservation of their faith amid blazing fires of hatred and persecution.

We know there were other manifestations amidst the period of great darkness which followed. What we call the Dark Ages, when a sort of fog came down on Christendom, were not without wonderful illumination here and there. Then, in a later period, God gave his great manifestation to Luther, and many things which had been slumbering awoke. Luther's message seems to have been a message of faith. He reawakened the principle that blessing and goodness are given by faith in Christ, as opposed to all that doctrine of works into which the Roman Church had stumbled.

There was also a very remarkable manifestation in the life and teaching of Calvin. He went astray in some respects, but he was seized with a marvellous understanding of divine things. His power lay in his perception of a certain factor in the nature of God, God's power to save, God's power to act in the moral nature independent of circumstances. We have that same idea in our own message. We also believe in the power of God to deal with the hidden things of the heart.

Then there came a very remarkable revelation through John Wesley. It had many distinct characteristics but the outstanding lesson was that of personal experience of God, the assurance of God's dealings with people. But it was more or less introspective. This revelation primarily led people to consider themselves, laying themselves bare before God as the great objects of his grace.[43]

And then came our message – the message to William Booth, summed up in one of his own great expressions: 'Saved to Save'.

Our Paul

Now, I say that this message from God did lead forward in a sense and direction which could not be said to have been true of previous messages. You say, what about the apostles? Well, at any rate I like to think that we are nearer the apostles than any of the religious teachers who have preceded us. When I think of my dear father I like to imagine him somehow or other intimately connected with Paul.

He was our Paul! There is much in his character which resembles Paul. Like the great apostle of the Gentiles, he was a bit sharp in his reproofs! Paul was one of the most hopeful, sanguine, beautiful of men, always believing that a thing would finish well. So was the old General. Paul was a great evangelist and a traveller for his evangelism, everlastingly on the move, never resting, never staying anywhere very long, always coming and going, and often going somewhere where nobody had been before. So with our dear old General. He was a ceaseless wanderer. He pushed his keel out on the waters of human ignorance and misery where no other keel had sailed before. Paul was both a great writer and a great talker, and the two things do not always go together. They did with Paul, and they did with William Booth. I prophesy that those who come after us will think more of William Booth's writings than we think of them.

There is much in the message given to us, in the call which has sounded through our hearts, similar to the message which came to the apostles. Like us they were up against godlessness. Like us, they encountered the stone walls of ignorance. They felt what we feel in our meetings a thousand times.

Oh, to know what we could do to reveal him so that these lost multitudes could look upon him! If only we can hold him up, he will draw all kinds of people to himself.[44]

Well, there we are. This is our work. There can be no doubt that the impulse which brought the Army into being was a divine impulse. It was not some strange human spasm which took possession of William Booth one day, and made him say that he of himself would do this thing. We know – especially those of us who knew him – that it was something not himself which urged him and pushed him and drew him and in a way almost drove him to seek those who were outside.

We say it was God. We say the impulse was divine. We say that the Holy Spirit chose his own vessels. For there were two. Catherine Booth was sick, and weak and in many ways delicate and shy, but she had a heart of fire. Her spirit, no doubt, fanned William Booth's spirit in many ways. She probably made him what he would never have been without her.

Yes, God chose his own vessels, first in our Founders, and then in those who gathered round them and followed them, all with the same token; all, having been saved themselves, were inspired with a great ambition for the salvation of others.

A man may be a good Catholic, or a good Presbyterian, or a good Methodist without being in any way pledged or bound to devote himself to the salvation of his fellows, but without that ambition no man can be a good Salvationist. It is vital that our leaders should recognise that. The solemn duty rests on us as leaders to make that principle felt everywhere among our people.

The test of the Bible

You may ask to what extent the Army[45] receives its divine direction and its dominating impulse from the Bible. Without going into any detailed answer to that question, on which a great deal might be said, I think the call comes to us, and has come from the first, outside the pages of the Bible. The message to those first Salvationists, while in harmony with the instructions of the Bible, was distinct from it.

Of course, like all revelations, it has to be taken to the test of the Bible. 'To the law and to the testimony: if they speak not according to this word, it is because there is no light in them' (Isaiah 8:20 *KJV*). That stands for every case. But as the old General used to say, we should be just as truly 'called' to our work for the souls of people, and just as truly commissioned to do it, if all the Bibles in the world ceased to exist tomorrow morning.

We should, of course, be weakened in our weapons. We should not have so good an armoury. We should miss one of the most wonderful sources of our strength. But we should, nevertheless, be called of God, and influenced by the Holy Spirit for the salvation of people through Jesus Christ our Lord.

How wonderfully our experience and history throughout the world confirm this! How wonderfully, in almost every country, we have seen repetitions of what took place in the first instance! We know how, all over the world, men and women have been spoken to by the Spirit of God, and sent out on various missions[46] of great difficulty, and have been placed in circumstances of extraordinary peril and extraordinary opportunity by the power of the Holy Ghost. And while there is always for us this grand test of the Word, yet it has been by the direct voice of God working in the hearts and minds of our people everywhere that we have seen some of the most wonderful results.

In this respect, again, does not our history harmonise with that of the first apostles? The early Christians had no New Testament Scriptures, only fragments, sometimes in the form of letters, which passed from one teacher to another, preserved sometimes more by accident than by design. It was not these things which had the greatest influence with them. It was the direct work of the Holy Spirit illuminating and sustaining their souls, quickening their stuttering tongues, enlarging their hearts, making them stronger than the fires of their persecutors.

And we ourselves have seen, both in the East and the West, but especially in the East, how closely our converts' warfighting has resembled that of the apostles, by the guidance and power of God. We have seen how similar to the apostles have been our difficulties and our triumphs when dealing with the ignorant, with people who have no idea of what we understand by 'education,' with people to whom Bibles are of no use because they could not read them if they had them, and people who, in some cases, cannot have a Bible because their language has not been brought to character, and has no marks to represent the sound. Yet how gloriously we have seen the Holy Ghost working among them!

The divine process in the Army

[47]All that we have seen accomplished can be directly traced to our evangelism, to getting everyone, everywhere, to know God. The divine endorsement of our message, in the evident fruit that grows everywhere people receive it, is sufficient testimony of its divine origin. One of the most encouraging facts in the whole history of Christianity is that the accomplishments of the Army are stamped with a veritable endorsement of God himself of his divine purpose in what we are doing, and his divine presence in our doing of it.

This is holy ground. Through insufficient agents, through untrained minds, through ignorant spirits, God has been working. Through the lowly things of the world and things which are despised, God has chosen to bring to nothing the things that are. He has stretched out his hand and touched us, he has confounded things that are mighty by his presence with the things that are not.

Only this morning I was reading a letter received from Trivandrum, South India, making some reports on particular aspects of the work about which I had asked. One illustration was of a man who, before his conversion, was wild and devil-possessed. And then he met the Army and salvation and became a new man, and his expression which struck me was, 'God touched me in my nakedness! God touched me!' And the officer writing the letter says, 'He has a marvellous holy influence over the people around him, though so ignorant and so rough; and that is the secret of it, dear General, with these people, many of whom cannot write or read their own names – God has touched them in their nakedness!'

The same kind of thing is seen elsewhere. We see it in the more educated communities of developed nations. Do we not see the alcoholic transformed out of his debauchery and beastliness?[48] God has touched him. Do we not see the doubter transformed? God has touched him! Do we not see the selfish and proud brought low in the service of his fellows? God has touched him!

The preparation of the messenger

The preparation of the *messenger* whom God has called is essential.[49] Here we are with this message. We are convinced of its truth and its efficacy.[50] We know that if we can only get it a hearing it will produce the most glorious results in human life. What we want is messengers to carry it out to the whole world. And God appoints some to be the preparers, the trainers, the shepherds, the 'stone-squarers' for the making of these messengers.

They must be suitable in character.[51] We sometimes say, 'God can use everybody.' But he cannot use 'any'body. Character is very important. We want them developed in ability. When we say 'ability' we do not necessarily mean intellectual power, or education, or worldly wisdom, we mean ability for the mission.[52] A person may be a great fool in many things and yet tread the highway of holiness, and be wise and skilful in our affairs.

We want them efficient in their own personal experience. They must themselves have heard and believed the message which they are sent out to tell to others. They must recognise that the message of salvation is a divine thing; that it is really from God. Many young people are in danger of tracing back the great things we have to teach them only to the Army.

Now, you know I am a Salvationist, and that out and out I believe in the Army. I believe that it is God's best up-to-date. I am a Salvationist all the way. But you know how futile it all is if we only lead people to the Army itself. We must make them, our learners, see that the message is from God. Some of them are lamentably dull at seeing spiritual things, awfully hard of hearing when it is a case of spiritual voices. We must be patient with the dull, the heavy, the slow. Yes, but we must teach them and teach them until they learn that the message they have to give is God's own.

Firstly, then, they must have heard themselves and believe. Second, they must recognise that the message of salvation is from God. Thirdly, they must know that the message is for the whole world.

I feel most strongly about each of these three matters. One of the great difficulties we come across when we get learners (of every nation) in the field is that often they have no great depth or root of conviction in themselves. It is not enough to be rooted in God, to have this knowledge of a divine Saviour, to have the mind illuminated and nature purified – even all that is not enough for those who have to stand up in battle alone. They must be possessed by this thing, absorbed by it, they must have conviction – the conviction that they are divine messengers, and that what they carry they carry from God himself. Let me beg of you to spare no pains to get this conviction into the heart of the individual learner.

A divided world

I am very anxious indeed that our young leaders should perceive the greatness of God's scheme of salvation. One of the great difficulties in the spread of Christ's work lies in the fragmentation of the world. All sorts of artificial divisions have been created, partly by the devil, no doubt, but partly as a result of circumstances which, in themselves, have no moral quality, good or bad.

We have to meet all sorts of artificial separations – separations which arise from the constitution of many countries. In many of the European countries there are purely artificial divisions. We are confronted with divisions resulting from extremes of wealth and of poverty. We have nations and tribes[53] cut off from one another by their own antagonistic habits and traditions. We have divisions of language, divisions that belong to climate, the divisions in some parts of the East that arise from caste. All these divisions comprise a watertight compartmentalisation that stifles our mission to spread to everyone the experience of knowing God personally.

But our message is for everyone, everywhere. We have the Word of life for every class, every language, every tribe, every nation, however widely separated, however differing, however averse. Hampering and dividing prejudices have always been a great obstacle to the dissemination of the message. But Jesus Christ, with a clear view of that difficulty, said, nevertheless, 'Go out and train everyone you meet, far and near, in this way of life...Then instruct them in the practice of all I have commanded you' (Matthew 28:19-20 *The Message*).[54]

The people who actually heard those words may all have been Jews. But you would not suggest that he intended to limit the application to Jews, that it was only the Jews who were appointed to be evangelists of the nations. No one would think that. He spoke to us all who have become his disciples – not only to those who were there at the time, but to those whom he knew would come after them. It was because he foresaw the great difficulty there would be in the spread of his message when it came to people other than those of his own nation, that almost his last words were the definite instruction, in case anyone be appalled by the challenge, and therefore abandon the mission,[55] 'Go into all the world and preach the gospel to all creation' (Mark 16:15).

Can we make each learner see that this message, this living Word, is for all peoples? Can we make them see – even as simple and ignorant youth – that in spite of their limitations, or poverty or ignorance, they possess the Pearl of Great Price? You may have a young lad, called from the stable, the field, the shop – to him is entrusted this message of life and hope.[56] He has in his hands, his heart, his mind, a divine message, given him, through The Salvation Army, by God himself. This message is one of incalculable enrichment to his own people; and not to them only, but to the people of every race, for whom he may be called to fight, for by this alone may people of every tribe[57] be saved.

One of the difficulties is the indisposition of younger leaders to leave their own land. They have no very definite interest in people outside their own frontiers. They are preoccupied with what is immediately around them. Overcome that provincialism in them as far as possible,[58] and make them see that this precious thing, the everlasting truth that God has entrusted to them, is for all peoples. The moment they feel global responsibility they will immediately question if they should do something. Little by little, God leading them, and you helping them, they will come to see that they have something God can use for the salvation of all people.⁵⁹

I know that some countries are different from others, and I am trying to talk of all. But what I am pleading for is that we should plant in the minds of these, our young messengers, the idea that what they have is for the whole world. It means catching a flame from the heart of God himself, who loved the whole world, and gave his Son to die for the whole world.

Is not that the most noble aspect of the love of God as we see it? It would be a completely different story if his love was merely for one set of people – people of one period in history, or people of one tribe or nation, or people of one social class, or people of this or that attitude towards him? It is the most amazing aspect of his love – that it is for the whole world. And this great truth reveals to us his benevolent character. How can you have a learner – or, for that matter, a leader – filled with the love of God and not overflowing with this universal compassion?⁶⁰

What a theme is ours! What a story we have to tell! What a message of love we have to spread! If the learners and the younger leaders could drink in a little more of the Calvary spirit of love for all people, if they could come nearer to the love of God in its wide reach and universality, it would empower them, not only in fighting overseas, but also on their local fronts among their own people.⁶¹ They will love their next-door neighbour not less, but better, if they also love people on the other side of the world.

Putting it high

You say to me, 'General, you are putting it high. You are asking a great deal of us.' I know I am, but I think I am back on the foundation facts of the love of God as seen in Christ, and I ask you to help me. I am trying to guide The Salvation Army to its great purpose, and I want you to inspire every learner so that he or she will assist the Army in its fulfilment.

We cannot know all about the material we have in our hands. We are not gifted with the inner sight which some of the old prophets seem to have possessed. The roughest and most uncouth and most unlikely people in our eyes often turn out to be the most useful. You do not know the kind of stuff you have got. It may be that the individual who seems the least likely of them all is just the one in whom the dry wood is ready laid to be fired by the thought that I have been trying to impart.

Do you say, 'I cannot hope to inspire every learner with this great ambition?' Well, even if you fail to convince some individuals of their own potential, maybe you can at least inspire them with this ambition for the Army. While certain individuals may never reach our Saviour's standard, at any rate, they may learn to fight, night and day,[62] in faith and prayer, with love and tears and enduring grace, to put the Army in that position to speak to all people so that, 'All may know he died for all.'

Reading Guide

General Bramwell Booth challenges us here on several levels. He argues that The Salvation Army has a unique message. A broad-stroke history of Christian revelation leads quickly to a peculiar message for Salvationists. He says we are 'Saved to Save'.

Now, this is no surprise to his first listeners. By 1925 the ubiquitous S's on uniforms of soldiers and officers around the world represented to everyone that the wearer was saved by Jesus to save everyone in the world. The passage of time has seen increased fuzziness around the uniform S's in the minds of Salvationists.

At some point between 1925 and today someone suggested that they 'really' mean 'saved to serve'. And *that* misreading subtly infiltrated the minds and mission of some Salvationists around the world, threatening to morph an effective great commission movement into a small 'c' Christian charity.

For the record, Bramwell Booth asserts that the Army's peculiar message is that we are 'Saved to Save'. It is the second saving component that distinguishes us from *some* ineffective churches and denominations on the one side, and non-government organisations and even 'faith-based' charities on the other.

Some might note that even official Salvation Army publications may have made the 'serve' mistake. Our quick response is, 'Is this allowed?'

This is a fundamental dictum of The Salvation Army. Can you slide in and decide to make other 'improvements'? Maybe you figure that the 'blood' in our slogan is a bit too gory and crude so you decide to 'improve' it, as a painter who once misread our motto and painted 'Flood and fire'. Is that legitimate?

Or what if 'ready to preach, pray or die at a moment's notice' just seems silly now so we 'improve' it to 'ready to help, hope or harm-reduce at a moment's notice'?

How can we change 'this is our speciality – getting saved, keeping saved and getting someone else saved', to 'getting served, keeping served, and getting someone else served'? Or, how can we change 'go for souls and go for the worst' to 'go for (government) service contracts and go for the biggest'?

It *sounds* a subtle difference. After all, the Army is famous for its effective service. And we intend to glorify God in and through our lives (sometimes through service). However, the result is a completely different mission:

- One is to save our family members; the other is to serve them.
- One is to save the marginalised; the other is to serve them.
- One is to save gross sinners; the other is to serve them.
- One is a salvation agency; the other is a service agency.
- One is to save the world (from sin); the other is to serve the world (in its sin).

So, an addict stumbles in off the street. 'Saved to Save' preaches the gospel as a means of becoming a new creation through Jesus' forgiveness and deliverance. 'Saved to serve' detoxes and teaches that he is a recovering addict forever.

And so on. Not only does mere service without salvation do a disservice to the ones served in that it leaves them bound for hell, but it does a disservice to our Lord who came to seek and to save us all. It ends up not helping us much either, in that we've proven disobedient and ineffective (if our service does not include the goal of saving).

Does 'Saved to Save' serve as well? Yes, of course.

Does 'Saved to serve' save as well? In many cases, yes. In some territories most conversions come from our rehabilitation centres. Praise God! But the saving is not guaranteed from that motto. General William Booth asserts: 'We are a salvation people – this is our speciality – getting saved and keeping saved, and then getting somebody else saved, and then getting saved ourselves more and more until full salvation on earth makes the heaven within, which is finally perfected by the full salvation without.'

Discussion Starters

1. 'Saved to save'? What do you think? Does it make a difference? Do we still have an 'unhealthy' passion for the salvation of our generation? If so, how is this expressed?

2. How is the uniqueness of our message played out in the daily warfare of The Salvation Army? How should it be played out?

3. How can mission be diverted? How can we thwart such diversions?

4. In this paper Bramwell Booth strongly argues that God cannot use just anybody. Character and preparation are important. How do you react to his claim? What processes can be put in place to match character with calling?

---

[32] *Training Staff Council Lectures 1925*, 'The Message and the Messenger', 3, IHQ, 1925.
[33] That is our great thought. We have what some religious people talk about as a 'concern' for the Salvation of our fellows.
[34] as He has dictated many means to effect... We find there that God's relations with men in the matter of their Salvation are described in various terms and under various characterizations.
[35] with that thought in mind...
[36] Perhaps the most striking of all the ideas involved in this effort or scheme or plan, is that the bringing of men to *the knowledge of God will be the remedy for their ills.*
[37] The New Testament has nothing plainer and simpler than the prayer of the Apostle, that we may 'know the love of Christ, which passeth knowledge.' We are to know Him, 'whom to know is life eternal.' Hallelujah!
[38] ...we are first and foremost charged with the duty of making God known. It is ours to bring about the fulfilment of some, at any rate, of these promises and directions. We have it specially laid upon us to extend the knowledge among men, not only of a Divine Father, but of a sufficient Saviour. So this our great business is to spread the knowledge of God. We have been raised up, equipped, sent forth, and maintained until this day by the power of the Holy Spirit that we may spread among men the knowledge of our Holy God and of Jesus Christ whom he has sent.

39 ...that main task. When we come closer to them, however, and see all that they are, we realise that every department...
40 ...the spreading of the knowledge of God.
41 *This paragraph is heavily abridged, but uses Bramwell Booth's own words.*
42 It was a message appropriate to their special condition and circumstance, and it had chiefly to do with the maintenance of the life which God had planted within them.
43 That had many characteristics peculiar to itself. Its outstanding lesson was that of personal realization of religion, the assurance of God's dealings with men. But it was more or less introspective. It was more or less a teaching which, in the main, led men to consider themselves, laying themselves bare before God as the great objects of His grace.
44 If only we can hold Him up, He will do the drawing!
45 The question may be asked how far The Army...
46 ...sent forth on various tasks...
47 *The next two paragraphs are heavily paraphrased, not just abridged.*
48 Is it not seen in the higher and more educated communities of the Western lands? Do we not see the drunkard transformed out of his debauchery and beastliness?
49 Now, my comrades, it is to the preparation of the *messenger* that God has called you.
50 ...wonderful effect.
51 We want them suitable...
52 ...work in hand.
53 ...and tribes... [*is not in the original text*].
54 We have the Word of life for every class, however widely separated, however differing, however averse. The hampering and dividing prejudices have always been a great obstacle to the carrying of the message. But Jesus Christ, with a clear view of that difficulty, said, nevertheless, 'Go ye therefore, and teach all nations' (Matthew 28:19 *KJV*).
55 ...task...
56 Can we make each Cadet see that this message, this Living Word, is for all peoples? Can we make him see–simple and ignorant youth as he may be–that in spite of his limitations, his poverty, his ignorance, he possesses the Pearl of Great Price? Lad as he is, called from the stable, the field, the shop, to him is entrusted this message of life and hope.
57 ...race...
58 They are occupied with what is immediately about them. I want you to overcome that provincialism in them as far as possible...
59 The moment they feel that responsibility with regard to the whole world there will arise in their minds some question as to whether they ought not themselves to do something; and, little by little, God leading them, and you helping them, they will come to see that they have something which can be used for the Salvation of all men.
60 How differently we should feel with regard to the nature of God Himself if His love were merely for one set of people–people of one period in history, or people of one race or nation... It is the grandest aspect of His love that it is for the whole world. How can you have a Cadet–or for that matter, an Officer–filled with the love of God unless he has something that answers to this universal compassion?
61 ...it would be a help to them, not only in doing work, perhaps, in lands beyond, but in doing work among their own people.
62 While he in himself may never reach the standard our Saviour set up, at any rate, he may learn to labour, night and day...

Chapter 3
Salvationism[63]
by Mrs General Florence Booth
International Training Staff Council 1925

SALVATIONISM is the sum total[64] of all that we can desire for our learners. The essence[65] of all that we desire for them is that they should be Salvationists. Whatever else we do for them during leader training, we must confirm and encourage them in uttermost devotion to The Salvation Army. They must be permeated with the spirit of Salvationism; our leader training would indeed be a dismal failure if it did not turn out Salvationists.

In these days when, in many of the countries where we are working, we have not the former difficulties of persecution, scorn and contempt, it is comparatively easy to become a Salvationist, and there is a danger of people coming in without really understanding the principles of The Salvation Army or what is involved in soldiership.

We need leaders who, before they enrol new people, will instruct them so that they will sign the articles of war understanding the principles of The Salvation Army, and will become true soldiers. It is vital that, in the training of learners, instruction in Salvationism should be emphatically clear. Your learners should have clearly before them those principles which have brought the Army into being and made it what it is. We know that some who come into our leader training system, truly consecrated and given to The Salvation Army, have a poor understanding of these principles. They have not been grounded in Salvationism. They do not realise the importance of the step taken by the Founder when he came out from his work for God as a minister of the Methodist New Connexion, to reach the down-and-out far outside the influence of the Christian Church. In some countries,[66] there is a tendency in some corps to sink back from that consecration of the Founder. Many soldiers act as if they were church members, coming to the Army for what they themselves receive, with little or no idea of service and responsibility for souls – willing to leave all the work to the officer.

Sometimes even officers sink into mere sermonisers; their time is almost entirely taken up by attending to the soldiers; their visiting, instead of being an aggressive attack on the souls of the people, is merely pastoral; they go from house to house among those who already belong to them. This tendency is disastrous, and the new leaders who go forth from training, instead of being drawn into this backwater, must act as an antidote to this drifting back and sinking tendency, and so help to keep The Salvation Army ship true to her course. They cannot do this unless their own hearts and minds are saturated with a clear understanding of Salvation Army principles. To effectively inculcate those principles you must consistently and continuously confront them with six aspects of Salvationism.[67]

1. The Founder secured for all who would have it a free expression of the joy of the Lord

In those days, as today, most Christians[68] felt that the affairs of the soul were private, very secret, not to be spoken about. How angry some people were in our holiness meetings when a Salvationist inquired as to their spiritual condition. They felt this was an intrusion on that which was sacred to themselves. The Founder saw clearly that the followers of Jesus should declare themselves, and that each of us should feel responsible to go and find out the spiritual condition of other people.[69]

This free expression of the joy of the Lord, such an important feature of The Salvation Army from its early days,[70] shows itself in testimony, freedom in prayer and separation from all worldly pleasures. Its gladness proves that we whose joy comes from Jesus do not need those avenues of false happiness and empty pleasure where people vainly seek satisfaction.[71] If we are to maintain this free expression of the joy of the Lord we must preserve in all its purity the first condition of membership of The Salvation Army given in those articles of war which every Salvationist has signed:

> *Having received with all my heart the salvation offered to me by the tender mercy of God, I do here and now publicly acknowledge God the Father to be my King; God the Son, Jesus Christ our Lord, to be my Saviour; and God the Holy Spirit to be my Guide, Comforter and Strength; and I will, by his help, love, serve, worship and obey this glorious God through time and through eternity.*

We must not allow this condition of service to slide. Leaders are responsible to see that it is understood and lived out, and to watch, for example, that the young people are not transferred to the senior roll unless they can sincerely subscribe to that first condition. There can be no second-hand spirituality among multi-generational Salvationists. We know there is a tendency in this direction. Young people must not be transferred from the juniors, and young adults must not be allowed to take up an instrument in the band, unless they give evidence of being truly converted and committed.[72]

Learners must be impressed with the importance of preserving this first condition of covenant community in The Salvation Army.[73] Some approaches to leader training can over-emphasise the importance of 'preaching'.

Yes, teach them to teach the people but it is essential to convince them to accept the fact that the primary means to reach other souls is the testimony of the soldiery and converts, as well as their own. During testimony periods, it is important to make sure that they give testimonies. Do not allow them to give little preachments with illustrations and accounts of their own doings, imagining that is testifying. Unless you are careful, the time for testimony may become merely an opportunity for learners to boast of their own deeds and speak of their own accomplishments. When you ask for testimonies explain that you want to hear only personal experience.[74]

The value of testimony should be preserved throughout the Army. This is your responsibility. Salvationism is neither comforting nor complete without testimony. Converts' testimony should be encouraged. I know in large meetings it is often impossible to let new converts testify on rising from the mercy seat, but in the smaller corps, and in some meetings in every corps, I think it important to let converts say at once what God has done for them. This committal of themselves greatly strengthens their faith.[75]

2. Faith in the possibility of holy living is a leading characteristic of Salvationism

I trust leaders everywhere realise the definite attack made by the devil on the holiness teaching and experience of the Army. How gloriously God taught and raised up the Founders when the light of this aspect of truth had become very dim! John Wesley, through whose writings the Founder himself was led into the experience of holiness, had been dead more than 70 years, and his followers were already beginning to neglect his teaching when the Army was born.

In some corps, how difficult it is to find among the soldiers and local officers *one* who gives testimony to holiness. How greatly the work of the Kingdom of God is hindered because of this lack in the corps, because of the inconsistency of some who profess to be Salvationists and yet are not separate from the world! The inefficiency of many corps as fighting forces is due to quarrelling, jealousies and bickerings amongst the soldiers. Holy living is the one cure for all that. It is evidence of lack of Holy Ghost power that so many of our people in their private lives accomplish so little for the salvation of souls, and lack holy courage and boldness to reprove sin.

The most many professing Salvationists do is to struggle to keep their own souls alive! They come to the meetings Sunday after Sunday and are refreshed, but go out to hide their light; whereas if they enjoyed this indwelling experience they would be aggressive, and soul winning would result.

I am a great believer in the personal influence of the individual. In many places we reap but little of the salvation of unbelievers because our people who live amongst those unbelievers are weak and powerless.

Lack of holiness experience is the chief cause of backsliding. What great progress the Kingdom of God would make in The Salvation Army if this could be checked! You can have significant influence on the Army's progress and well-being by featuring holiness in your leader training. We need young leaders to clearly understand God's purpose for all of us to be holy. They must be determined to make their holiness teaching effective. Make it clear to them that the theory in the mind that does not advance to become experience in the heart is poison.[76]

3. Salvationism includes definite responsibility for the souls of others

Leaders who fail to impress this responsibility for souls on their soldiers fail in raising a salvation people. The Salvation Army is a band of war fighters,[77] a union of soul winners. When the Founders gathered people around them, it was to get people saved, discipled, trained and deployed. Listen to the Founder[78]:

> In the providence of God, I was led to make certain efforts to bring the poor people living in the eastern parts of London to a knowledge of God and into the enjoyment of the salvation provided for them by Jesus Christ...I hoped that I might be able to benefit the people around me, and, though calculating that a certain force of helpers would be raised up to cooperate with me, I had no anticipation of the expansion of the work I had taken in hand beyond the neighbourhood in which it was commenced. Great crowds of the working people came to hear me talk, a large number were convinced of sin by the Holy Ghost, and many of them responded to my invitations to come to Christ for salvation... Much enthusiasm was created, and many of the converts became my co-workers. These I met regularly every week, personally instructing them in the things of God, counselling them in the difficulties they had to contend with, and showing them how to do the work they had undertaken.

These people were gathered around the Founder to be his co-workers. This describes a typical corps today,[79] the soldiers and local officers grouped together normally under the leadership of the officer, to be his or her co-workers. When that is the reality, a small force will make a profound impression on a very large number of people.

All Salvationists should feel a clear responsibility for the salvation of souls, whether or not they have or will have any connection with The Salvation Army. God will give to the Army those whom he calls and fits as workers. We must never let our soldiery think that they should only try to get people saved who can benefit the Army, and who will become Salvationists.[80] When that spirit comes into a corps, you will find that the soldiers give the cold shoulder to down-and-outs, to the people who they feel will reflect no credit on them. They are afraid to bring the neediest, for whom indeed we exist, into association with us. Wherever such soldiers are, the Army spirit is watered down.

Therefore, raise up young leaders[81] with a genuine desire for the salvation of the ungodly, apart altogether from whether or not their connection with The Salvation Army is going to shed any lustre on their warfare. Help your learners to realise that the focus of their fighting is in the salvation of souls even when this will not add to the soldiership of The Salvation Army. Soul-saving is our purpose.

Deploy leaders who will raise fighting soldiers, and those leaders will reap a huge harvest, although they[82] themselves can come into touch with comparatively few people. The corps with 50 soldiers who really love God and are soul winners, is in touch with tens of thousands.

In a word, if we are to be 'Salvation Army', we must have leaders who can be true to the pattern given by the Founder. Such leaders will contribute to the true life-blood of the Army. In season and out of season they will seek those for whom God raised up the Army.

4. One of the most striking features of The Salvation Army is that woman has a position secured to her

It is very important that all our leaders should understand what The Salvation Army has accomplished for women. Briefly stated, the Army's attitude to woman is that it gives her, in every office or position to which she may be appointed, an absolute equality with man. The status of a woman field officer is the same in every sense as that of a man field officer. I do not say that the Army places every women on an equality with every man, any more than it places any one woman on an equality with every other woman.

No one would say, for example, that every one of our women captains would be fit for the opportunities for which some of them are suited. Some women captains are not fit for the positions that some men captains occupy, and vice versa; but every opportunity which is open to man in The Salvation Army is open to woman. If she has the necessary gifts, there is nothing in the constitution of the Army, or in its principles or laws, which would close the door of any position in it to a woman because of her sex. This principle has been worked out by the Army – which puts into practice what it teaches – to such an extent that wherever we look closely into the history of the Army and examine its work, we find the power of woman, the influence of woman, the devotion of woman. Taking the Army as a whole, women and men have played an equal part in it.

In Salvation Army positions, women have authority over men just as men have similar positions of authority over women. There was a great battle for this in the early days. When the Founder first established this principle, men of all kinds objected to being commanded by women. The Founder, the Army Mother, and the present General united to fight this battle out. They saw there could be no half way; and that it would be an inconsistent rule that gave woman responsibility and yet withheld authority; and so the battle was fought out. It is difficult for us today to understand the originality and the courage which enabled the Founders to establish this position for women in the Army at a time when the position of women was altogether different in the world at large from what it is today.

John Stuart Mill's pamphlet, *The Subjection of Women* (one of the first volumes published in the woman's cause) appeared in 1869 [it was republished by Dover Thrift Editions in April 1997], four years after the birth of The Salvation Army . I wonder whether he knew, at the time, of the Founder's effort. How powerless were his clever arguments and clear reasoning to accomplish anything in the cause for which he wrote!

That first pamphlet passed out of print, and nothing was heard of it for years until a new issue was made during the battle of women for freedom preceding the late war. When that pamphlet was first published, the Founder had already brought into being a concrete example of that for which Mill contended in words. This illustrates the importance of bringing all our teaching into action. Mere theories can so soon become dead and useless, clogs in the wheels of progress.

In the Western countries the social and legal enfranchisement of woman has made great strides latterly; but there is still much ground to win. Many legal difficulties remain, and there will be much for which to contend and suffer before woman's complete enfranchisement is secured. This progress, or lack of progress, has not affected woman's position in the Army. The political enfranchisement of women has not affected us, for instance, for the position of woman was secured in the very constitution of the Army. The Founder firmly planted the foundation principle of the equality of the sexes.[83]

Make it plain to learners that the equality of the sexes is established in the Army in three important directions:

1. In spiritual privilege. God is no respecter of persons. His power and his Spirit are given to women as well as to men. At Pentecost the gift of the Holy Ghost was bestowed upon woman equally as upon man; and so today he, the Holy Ghost, fits a woman to work for God and take her place as an officer, local officer or soldier in the Army.

2. In equality of responsibility. Whatever position a woman holds in the Army the responsibilities of that position are identical for her as for a man in that same position.

3. In equality of opportunity and authority. These are leading principles of The Salvation Army. I ask you to impress upon your learners that, as leaders, they will be called upon to carry them out. *I hope you realise that this battle is not yet entirely won, and that even within the ranks of The Salvation Army a good deal of prejudice still remains.* There are many who, even though they may not be inclined to dispute the theory of woman's equality, yet hold back in practice.

Many among the women are only too ready to accept the position won for them by the Army Mother and the women of the past, without carrying any responsibility for the maintenance of that position. They shrink from the sacrifice involved. The women must claim their position and shoulder its burdens. They must not shrink back before any prejudice they may meet from the men among whom they fight. What the Army has a right to look for in its women is sympathy with womanhood. They must take the women's side and honour the women's position among men.

What a debt we owe to the Army Mother! She won this position for us. I wish I had time to say more about her. It was the greatest privilege of my life to be associated with her, and to know something of the great cross to her retiring, nervous nature when she stood forth as one of those first public women. How anxious she was that all our women should have courage to do that, and yet preserve their womanliness! Had the Founder allied himself to a woman of inferior mind and weak character, how very different the history and character of the Army might have been!

5. The spirit of internationalism is a part of Salvationism which must be fostered among your learners

Guard them from a narrow outlook. This is very important, for the unity and well-being of the Army as a whole depend very largely on the international spirit of its leaders. We cannot live for one people alone if we accept our commission from the captain of our salvation: 'But you will receive power when the Holy Spirit comes on you; and you will be my witnesses in Jerusalem, and in all Judea and Samaria, and to the ends of the earth' (Acts 1:8).

We are not all called to go as missionaries to other lands, but if the spirit of Christ possesses our leaders, they will not lack desire to help Christ's cause in every possible way beyond the borders of their own narrow interests and their own homeland. The international spirit in its leaders is vital to The Salvation Army. What difficulties arise when leaders look on their own things only, instead of accepting the whole world as their responsibility,[84] and feeling as much interest in and care for the success of the corps across borders as for their own! Their outlook affects the work of The Salvation Army in their district, to say nothing of the larger and wider sphere of the global warfare,[85] and work done to meet the various needs of the people throughout the world. May God help us to fan the fire and keep the flame of internationalism burning throughout the Army!

6. True Salvationism includes loyalty

The word 'loyalty' is very beautiful in every language. As the dictionary defines it, loyalty means true or faithful allegiance; keeping faith; constant in service, devotion, and regard. Loyalty includes the idea of love. The word is used especially in speaking of allegiance to a sovereign, government or country, but it can be applied also in all relationships of trust and confidence. The loyalty of its leaders has been fundamental to the success of The Salvation Army. *This spirit of loyalty must be breathed into the learners in order that they may succeed in the following directions:*

Learners should be true to themselves

Our service in The Salvation Army is especially marked by pledges. Soldiership involves putting our hand to the covenant of the articles of war[86] – the pledge of allegiance to the foundation doctrines of the Army; the pledge as to conditions of service, including the total abstinence pledge, the pledge of obedience, the pledge of separation from the world.

We are rightly very proud of the total abstinence pledge, but I sometimes wonder whether it holds too large a place in the outlook of our people. Even though there may be grave inconsistencies in their own lives, very few will tolerate the breaking of that pledge. If someone who has been a drunkard falls under sudden temptation, how ready are the soldiers to rip off his epaulettes.[87] But some other of our pledges involve far more important principles, the pledge of separation from the world, for instance. A soldier true to that pledge will certainly abstain from strong drink, but will also abstain from a lot of other negative activity and engage in a lot of positive activity.[88]

A special feature of Salvation Army service and Salvationism is that we are such a highly-pledged people. Local officers are pledged further than soldiers, and the young people received into the training colleges as cadets are pledged still further. Solemn pledges are demanded of them as to the disposal of their time, as to courtship and marriage, in addition to a renewal of allegiance to Salvation Army doctrines, principles and methods.[89] The history of the Army has abundantly justified us in demanding these pledges, but we must inculcate loyalty and honesty, and train our learners to carry out what they have undertaken and accepted in principle.

It is of the utmost importance that learners should realise the extent to which they are covenanted,[90] and the importance to themselves of loyalty to those pledges. Let them understand that their fidelity and integrity[91] are at stake. To be untrue to others is disastrous. To be untrue to oneself is to betray one's better nature. To make certain pledges when called by God, when the standard is raised and accepted, and then to break those pledges, is destructive of character. The words spoken by Polonius in William Shakespeare's *Hamlet* apply here: 'To thine own self be true…thou canst not then be false to any man.'

Salvation Army learners[92] must be possessed by a spirit of love and fidelity towards God and their leaders, a spirit of devotion to their warfighting in the Army. They must definitely be willing to submit to regulations and to prefer the interests of God and his work as manifested in the Army to their own. This spirit is of more value than any special powers, gifts or graces. Those possessed by it will render service that will be rewarded in the day of crowning service of which the Saviour will say, 'Well done, good and faithful servant! You have been faithful with a few things; I will put you in charge of many things' (Matthew 25:21).

Loyalty to pledges made to God and the Army in moments of high inspiration, brings unity with the whole Salvation Army and access to its anointing and strength.[93]

Learners should set up a standard of loyalty to others

Teach them that true loyalty is something more than fidelity, it is fidelity and love.

Loyalty is not a virtue that can be self-contained. It involves more than one individual. Relationships in the Army world are complex, and if the real unity so necessary to the strength and preservation of the

Army is to be preserved, the spirit of loyalty throughout our ranks is very important. It is important that your learners should set up a standard of loyalty with regard to the personal ties, relationships and friendships in their lives. How important is loyalty in that wonderful unit of Salvation Army service, the corps: loyalty between soldier and captain, between captain and lieutenant, between commanding officer and divisional staff. There must be loyalty in carrying out instructions, loyalty in preserving the reputations of others, loyalty which makes us in honour to prefer one another.

How much unnecessary loss arises when officers who follow one another in charge of the different corps fail in loyalty to their predecessor and care, for instance, less about the converts they find there than about their own converts, and are not enthusiastic about maintaining new initiatives on new fronts, such as the scouts and guards, because they have not had credit for inaugurating them at the corps. What a lack of loyalty to their predecessor!

Bacon has said, 'Use the memory of thy predecessor fairly and tenderly; for if thou dost not, it is a debt will sure be paid when thou art gone.' Aim for the significant accomplishment in leader training of establishing in the minds and hearts of young leaders the importance of loyalty in personal relationships.[94]

Implant in our learners the loyalty of submission to the Army and to Army regulation

Loyalty is the expression of a certain spirit on the part of one who serves, to the one to whom service is rendered. In my mind, true loyalty to any cause may be compared to patriotism. We all have a glowing idea of what true patriotism, love and devotion to a country should mean. There can be no true patriotism without willingness to subordinate personal and individual interests to the well-being of the country; no true love of country without willingness to serve. The love of a Salvationist to the Army is of the same nature as true patriotism. A man's well-being is wrapped up with the well-being of his country. A man who, in time of war, steps into the ranks to defend his country, defends his own homestead and his own dear ones at the same time. The existence and spiritual prosperity of The Salvation Army are intimately connected with the existence and well-being of the true Salvationist; and those who stand bravely to defend the Army and its principles undoubtedly defend their own well-being and their own opportunities in the service of God.

To the true Salvationist, The Salvation Army cannot merely be an alternative manner and method of serving God and the people. It must be something more than that. Learners are under no compulsion to serve in The Salvation Army, but if they choose to so serve, it is very important that they shall be true patriots. In my reading this morning I read again those words in the epistle to the Hebrews that seem so wonderfully to express Salvation Army patriotism: 'People who say such things show that they are looking for a country of their own. If they had been thinking of the country they had left, they would have had opportunity to return. Instead, they were longing for a better country – a heavenly one. Therefore God is not ashamed to be called their God, for he has prepared a city for them' (Hebrews 11:14-16).

These words continually rejuvenate the spirit as they apply to this dwelling place called The Salvation Army, this place he prepared for our service when he called us out,[95] and made us feel, 'Your people will be my people and your God my God' (Ruth 1:16).

The true spirit of Salvationism looks upon service in The Salvation Army after that fashion: it is a spirit of love for the Army making any other avenue of service impossible. If Abraham had been hankering after the lifestyle of his old country, he might also have started looking for the opportunity to return.[96] The same could be said of our Founders, and the pioneer officers of The Salvation Army.

Loyalty is still the same,
Whether it win or lose the game;
True as the dial to the sun,
Although it be not shined upon.
    Samuel Butler (1835-1902)

Reading Guide

Florence Booth lays out the principles of Salvationism forcefully in this piece. She outlines six features of Salvationism:

1. Free expression of the joy of the Lord.
2. Faith in the possibility of holy living.
3. Definite responsibility for the souls of others.
4. A position for [i.e. the equality of] women.
5. Spirit of internationalism.
6. Loyalty.

This list might surprise some readers. In some parts of the developed world it could be argued that few of these dynamics are prevalent. Free expression has been dulled by inheritance of grandparents' faith and an ingrafted alien subculture of propriety. Faith in holy living has been stunted by contrary teaching and complacent experience. Responsibility for souls has been delegated to leaders. Beyond the corps, a woman's leadership role has been almost pervasively marginalised (to women-only ministries, beyond the corps). Internationalism has been supplanted by local commitment that evidences the fragmentation of the Western Army. Loyalty has been replaced by convenience.

Where this is happening, Salvationism has been reduced to an inoffensive, innocuous, generic brand of Protestantism that seems practically useless. Florence Booth's teaching provides the solution. If we read and apply her lessons here, then we have started the path back to our dangerous roots.

Principles are important in a book on training leaders. Otherwise, we reduce the whole exercise to 'scientific management', outlining a series of standardised actions to elicit set consequences. Training leaders is much more than surface actions. It is more than 'one-minute managers' and 'management by walking around' and the other trendy 'how-to' formulae for landing the next big promotion. The principles undergirding both tactics and strategies must be owned by the leaders being trained. When your learners embrace the principles, that list from Florence Booth makes sense.

Discussion Starters

1. From your Salvation Army perspective, how do you relate to Florence Booth's list of principles?

2. How can these features of Salvationism be inculcated into those you train?

3. Discuss each of the six features in terms of its effectiveness in your leadership setting.

---

[63] *Training Staff Council Lectures 1925*, 'Salvationism', 85, IHQ, 1925.
[64] …summing up…
[65] …kernel…
[66] Especially in the older countries…
[67] This they will not do unless in their own hearts and minds there is a clear understanding of Salvation Army principles. If you are to present those principles to them, it will be necessary to keep continually before them six aspects of Salvationism.
[68] In those days, as at present, most religious people…
[69] …each should feel responsible to go forth and inquire after the condition of other people.
[70] …so marked a feature of The Salvation Army from the first…
[71] …people seek a satisfaction not to be found.
[72] *The original does not contain the words 'and committed'.*
[73] Cadets must be impressed with the importance of preserving this first condition of membership in The Salvation Army.
[74] It is right to impress them with the need to teach the people; but it is imperative that we shall help them to understand and accept the fact that the principal avenue through which to reach other souls is the testimony of the Soldiery and Converts, and of their own lips.

When testimonies are called for from the Cadets, it is worth while taking care that they give testimonies… Cadets should never be allowed to preach to one another in a Testimony Meeting: they should never be allowed to preach at all at other Cadets, or to admonish them or boast about what they themselves are doing. Unless care be taken, the time for testimony may become merely an opportunity for Cadets to boast of their own deeds and speak of their own accomplishments. There are proper times, of course, when you can give them an opportunity to speak of what they are accomplishing for souls; but that is not testimony. When you ask for testimonies explain that personal experience must be rigidly adhered to.

[75] *This paragraph is heavily abridged, omitting Florence Soper's (Mrs General Bramwell Booth's) testimony of her first contact with The Salvation Army and her comments on uniform-wearing, but closely retaining her own words.*
[76] Here the Training Garrison can accomplish a work which will have the most far-reaching consequences in the Army's progress and well-being. I ask you to send the young Officers forth with a distinct understanding of this purpose of God that man shall be holy. Send them forth determined to make the Holiness Meetings really helpful. Make it clear to them that the right theory in the mind, which does not become a cardinal experience, is like a poison.
[77] …workers…
[78] Soul-winning, and the development of Converts, were the objects of the Founders when they

79 That is typical of what a Corps should be today…
80 We must never let our Soldiery think that they are to seek the Salvation only of those who will be profitable to The Army, and who will become Salvationists.
81 Therefore send forth from your Garrisons young Officers…
82 Help the Cadets to realise that their work is the Salvation of souls even when this will not add to the soldiership of The Salvation Army. Soul-saving is our work.

    Send forth Officers who will raise fighting Soldiers, and those Officers will reap a multitude, although they…
83 *Mrs Booth was speaking in 1925.*
84 What difficulties arise when a Field Officer looks on his own things only, instead of accepting the whole world as his parish…
85 …Missionary Work…
86 …pledges laid down in the Articles of War…
87 …to turn him out neck and crop…
88 He who is true to that pledge will certainly abstain from strong drink, but he will also abstain from, and perform, a good deal else.
89 *A section relating to corps officers visiting people in their homes is omitted here.*
90 …pledged…
91 …sincerity…
92 The young people who go forth annually to the service of The Army…
93 …means partaking of its strength.
94 No mean work will be accomplished in the Training Garrison if loyalty in personal relationships can be set up in the hearts and minds of the young Officers who pass out each year.
95 Those words have continually come to my own heart with power as applied to this dwelling place The Salvation Army, this place He had prepared for our service when He called us out…
96 Truly, if Abraham of old had been mindful of his former country, he might also have been mindful of the opportunity to return.

Chapter 4
The Ethos of Leader Training[97]
by Mrs General Florence Booth
International Training Staff Council 1925

MY subject is the spirit which should possess those training learners and turning them into leaders. The word is inadequate for my purposes, and yet I fancy you know what I mean by spirit.[98]

It is evident that our leader training can be controlled and possessed by a certain spirit. Many organised undertakings are seen to be possessed by a distinctive spirit, a spirit appropriate to them. In a well-officered ship a certain spirit possesses the crew. In every business a spirit, good or bad, honest or dishonest, rules, and is well known to all in that business.

One of our candidates left a good business post because she felt the advertising was dishonest. Bonuses were promised on a generous scale to shareholders, but she knew the first bonus, quickly given, would not be followed by others. A people, representing all kinds of temperaments and character and widely different views, may be animated as one person by one spirit, the spirit of nationality, the spirit of ambition. An army, large or small, may be possessed in all ranks by a certain spirit which makes it invincible or which marks it for defeat.

I think no one will question that The Salvation Army, as a whole, is possessed of a certain spirit. Though manifested in a different measure in different circumstances, and by the various units which make our Army, that spirit is a great fact, perhaps the great outstanding fact about us. Distinctions of race, nationality, character, intellectual development, upbringing, are all more or less neutralised by the spirit which possesses the whole organisation. In a lesser degree, a distinctive spirit may pervade a corps. While at one with the sprit of the whole Army, it may develop a life, a passion, a spirit all its own not to be found in another corps.

An organised and specific[99] enterprise, such as our leader training in each country, can and should be possessed of one and the same spirit in every land. That spirit should be a manifestation of all that is best in The Salvation Army. How difficult is definition when we come to the things of the Spirit! But surely the spirit which should govern leader training is a manifestation of the Spirit of God seen in:

1. Spiritual fervour.
2. Devotion to principle.
3. Uttermost consecration to the great ends the Army has in view.

I think if we claim these three initial factors as being the inner impulse of our leader training we shall not be far wrong. It will be your highest aim to inspire, maintain, and cultivate that spirit.

It is imperative that this spirit should capture your learners and manifest itself in them. Indeed, that to which all your work for them should lead is to inspire them with this same spirit. How vital the spirit of life is to all our work! I appeal to you, my dear comrades, to do everything you can to help us in this matter.

Looking at the men and women who have accomplished lasting impact in the Army, especially in difficult fields, but whom we did not regard as having special gifts or qualifications,[100] we often try to explain it in some such manner: [101]'Oh, it was something in the personality...There was an atmosphere about him...She had a way with her.' It was the spirit which animated him, the spirit she showed; this is what we have really meant in each case.

No matter what the achievements of our leader training may be, no matter what its perfections or imperfections may prove to have been when the young leaders are thrust into the actual hurly-burly of conflict, the effectiveness of its foundation work in character will depend upon the spirit which possesses the whole enterprise. I do not want to overdo[102] this, and yet this is perhaps the moment when I should emphasise the fact that nothing can be successfully substituted for this spirit.

This is self-evident when we consider the work of our training systems as a whole. None of our training staffs throughout the world would question that unless a certain spirit possess the training effort, that effort will fall far short of its aim. And yet I need to impress on you the necessity to carry this spirit into each of the distinct activities of the different systems. No training system is possessed and governed by this spirit unless this spirit dominates each accountability meeting, each field deployment, each debrief and finds expression in every arrangement and decision belonging to the war.[103]

Learners cannot feel that their training as a whole is possessed of the right spirit if the interviews of one leader are merely mechanical, or if this or that class is no different from a class in a secular school, and, far from being charged with the spirit of which I am thinking, has no spirit in it at all.[104]

God's government is a paternal government. He seeks to inspire his children with the spirit of the heavenly Home, with the benevolence of true love which would make them instruments to bring about people's highest good. Every department of Salvation Army service must manifest the benevolence of love, the desire to impart the highest good.

A temptation sometimes assails our young leaders to feel they are merely made use of, that the very most is squeezed out of them, and that their intimate well-being, their personal life, is lost sight of. And, frankly,[105] don't their leaders occasionally open the door to this temptation? Ours is a war, I know, and in war sacrifice is required. But our warfare is different from military warfare in that we need not ask any sacrifice from our warriors that is not equally for their own highest good as for the good of the cause.

With us, 'Whoever loses their life for me will find it' (Matthew 16:25). Benevolence should possess leader training. If true benevolence prevails, your learners will feel that their own highest good is not sacrificed to realise the highest good of the Army to which they belong.[106]

Sincerity

'Sincerity' is derived from Latin, and is very full of meaning; taken literally it means 'without wax'. Sculptors were in the habit of filling in the flaws in marble with wax – well matched and difficult to detect.

But if the statue was exposed to the weather, the sun melted the wax and discovered the fraud. Hence the meaning – freedom from pretence. It is vital that learners and leaders be sincere. The presence or absence of sincerity can make all the difference between value and worthlessness in character. In the training system, sincerity is the one talisman that can protect against the evils of hypocrisy, fanaticism and mere profession.

The training college cannot but be a spiritual hothouse,[107] and in some respects the life of the learners is very unnatural because their minds to a very great extent are held in one direction. Much praying, singing and listening to talks on religious subjects, personal interviews, continual exhortations to self-examination, recurring spiritual days – all this gives rise to dangers against which we must intelligently seek to guard our learners as a body and individually. It is more or less bewildering, too, to be plunged into a life so strange and new.[108]

I wish we could order our training systems, in respect to freedom, after the fashion of colleges so that, apart from the actual classes or lectures, the learners could be absolutely free – but perhaps that cannot be. I give that as a thought of my own. It is vital that as much time, freedom and room as possible should be allowed the learners for the natural expression of their own personality.

For many years I had the care of the social institutions for women in Britain, and I know that the idea of some officers in institutions is to make rules and regulations for the relief of the officers rather than for the benefit of the inmates. I believe that policy prevails in some training systems, and wherever it prevails there is sure to be a suppression of the individual learner, which is detrimental to the true spirit of sincerity and to the true interests of training.

Am I claiming too much when I say that the spirit of sincerity can possess a people such as we have in leader training systems, only when those people have intelligently and definitely set out to train themselves in sincerity; when they are watchful, and determined to allow nothing in themselves that would hinder sincerity?

The glorious salvation of God provides for sincerity. Holy people know that God desires sincerity before all else in his children, and are horrified at the thought of falling short in sincerity.[109] 'Surely you desire truth in the inner parts,' cried David (Psalm 51:6 *NIV 1984*). God desires to make of us a people true, through and through; a people whose hearts are possessed by love of truth and frankness, and whose consciences are tender about any misrepresentation or sham.

It is very important that, when dealing with learners in personal interviews and at all times, leaders should place a true value on sincerity. They should be very watchful not to give praise to those learners who are more showy, and look instead to affirm those whose character outweighs their gifts and skills. Leaders need to encourage and appreciate these people.[110] You realise that sincerity is an important characteristic of the spirit that should reign in the leader training system.

Justice

Another characteristic which should mark leader training is justice. The spirit of leader training will in part proceed from, and be manifested in, the government of the system. No government can be good that does not exercise justice; for justice is one of the chief ends of government. Justice is essential in leader training. It is not detrimental to that benevolence which desires the highest good of your learners.

Love and justice convey to our mind the highest idea of moral good. Love and justice are not necessarily mutually inclusive, for it is possible to love without being just, and it is certainly possible to administer justice without love. But, when they are found together, love and justice enhance each other. Love strengthened by justice is rendered infinitely more valuable, and justice tempered with love becomes infinitely more powerful.

To think justly, to decide justly, to act justly, manifests enlightenment of mind and realisation of the rights of others. Ignorance, darkness, lack of understanding make justice impossible. A true grasp of facts, the power to see things as they are, is necessary to all who would be just, decide justly, and act with justice. God requires that we should be just: 'He has shown you, O mortal, what is good. And what does the Lord require of you? To act justly and to love mercy and to walk humbly with your God' (Micah 6:8).

Injustice is a source of suffering worldwide. How often the happiness of little children is blighted because of injustice! Beginning domestically and then looking out globally,[111] what violations of the rights of others, what cruelties, what bitterness we see brought about through lack of justice! The darkness of sin obscures justice and encourages people to fix their eyes on their own rights, and to ignore the rights of others: to see only what is due to them from other people, and to be altogether blind to what is due from them to others.

Think about justice! It is a fascinating subject, for God himself is just, and man at his best is always just. This is one of those unmistakable stamps of the likeness of God on the human heart. We were created in the image of God to be just. When God's image is restored in us, then we shall be just.

Every heart craves for justice. In the most ignorant, in the most degraded, when almost every virtue is obscured, a desire for justice can be found. The cry for fair play will touch the most lawless. The triumph of sin is described by the prophet in these remarkable words: 'No one calls for justice; no one pleads a case with integrity' (Isaiah 59:4). This is the uttermost darkness of the human soul.

We can realise much of what justice is by searching our own hearts, for God has implanted justice within us. But let us above all search our knowledge of him, for in him alone is absolute justice to be found. 'Righteousness and justice are the foundation of your throne; love and faithfulness go before you' (Psalm 89:14).

When justice is mentioned in the Bible, mercy is often coupled with it because the justice of God is always associated with mercy and truth. Our Saviour's golden rule makes justice most easily understood: 'Do to others as you would have them do to you' (Luke 6:31).

Justice is essential to the success of your training work. The training leaders, from the highest to the lowest, are administrators of justice; and, without just dealing and just thinking on the part of the individual leader, justice cannot be truly said to govern the training work as a whole.

In asking you to guard against injustice, I need not allude to the extremes of injustice, such as cruelty; but I appeal to you who have the well-being of leader training systems in your hands to be watchful against injustice.

I appeal for fairness, for equity, in the treatment of learners. One case of failure in justice would hinder all your efforts.[112] It does not take much ink to stain a glass of pure water; a drop will do it. So in leader training, lack of justice in one detail of your administration, lack of justice shown by one subordinate leader, will do a great deal to mar the spirit which governs the system and to destroy the confidence of your learners. Unless the spirit of justice in training be fostered with watchful care, contrary spirits will very easily stick themselves out.

Favouritism, for instance, is *destructive of justice*. The slightest approach to favouritism in dealing with learners is disastrous. Do all you can by means of example, and by direct teaching as far as is necessary, to show the young leaders, whom it is your duty to train for their work, that favouritism would mar the spirit that should govern the training.

Teach them the importance of rigid self-control in this matter. Do not tell them that they are not to have favourites, because that would be impossible. Human beings cannot but feel preferences. For instance, one person's favourite flower is the rose, another prefers the lily. Help your young leaders to see that they are not to be condemned for having preferences, but that they will merit utmost condemnation if they let favouritism govern their judgement, be seen in their looks and actions, and heard in their words.

Prejudice is equally destructive of justice.[113] The devil is tremendously opposed to us in our endeavour to send forth young people fitted and equipped as Salvation Army leaders. He is as busy in the training system of The Salvation Army as anywhere, because such important issues are involved, and because he makes definite, persistent efforts, to spoil every consecrated life.

The training leaders must be watchful not to allow prejudice to warp their own judgement, watchful to warn young leaders against this evil. Prejudice on the part of leaders in favour of those they like, and prejudice against those whom humanly speaking they would dislike, must not be allowed in training systems. It would work havoc there.

Remember that we do not want to turn out leaders of one pattern – the pattern that appeals particularly to you. That type of leader may be very useful, but so also may be the type of leader who is good and sincere, but for whom you have less preference.

If prejudice against a learner exists, it is injurious even if it is not known to that learner personally. It cuts off from that learner the help he ought to have; it influences the other leaders against him, and the power of the training system to help that particular learner is brought almost to naught.

Leaders should regard the capacity to be just and to deal justly as a precious gift of the Holy Spirit. All training leaders should cultivate in themselves, and foster in others, a love of justice, watchfulness on behalf of justice, and a determination not to be biased by favouritism or prejudice.[114]

Obedience

Another characteristic of the spirit which should rule in the training system is obedience. Government and discipline constitute a very important part of The Salvation Army; and it is essential that learners should understand the meaning of Salvation Army discipline before they become leaders. The Army Mother said: 'Obedience to properly constituted authority is the foundation of all moral excellence.'

Looking back over 44 years of officership, it seems to me impossible to speak too highly of the value and importance of Salvation Army discipline. During nearly six years of work as British Commissioner (BC) [Territorial Commander (TC) of the United Kingdom with the Republic of Ireland Territory] I realised very clearly that if all leaders had a truer idea, a stricter ideal, of obedience to rules and regulations, a much greater advance would be made throughout the Army world. Some heart-breaking catastrophes came before me which would certainly have been avoided if there had been no departure from Salvation Army discipline, rule and regulation.

How many officers break the regulation which demands that there shall always be more than one person present when money is counted! The breaking of this rule makes an entry for temptation where there would otherwise be no temptation. Some officers have fallen before particular temptation, from which, had they but kept the regulation, they would have been protected. I have known accusations, sometimes false, made against officers who have disregarded the regulation about courtship, and about having people of the opposite sex in the quarters, and so have not protected themselves from evil tongues, or, indeed, from actual disaster.

We must not be too quick to say that our military titles are merely titles and that our government is not military. The Army government is paternal and on the family plan, but let's not lose the strengths of military organisation in unified action. Learners will realise permanent benefit from our imposition of obedience in the training system.[115]

Obedience is one of the foundation principles of God's government. What gracious promises are attached to obedience! 'Now if you obey me fully and keep my covenant, then out of all nations you will be my treasured possession' (Exodus 19:5).

'If you listen carefully to what he says and do all that I say, I will be an enemy to your enemies and will oppose those who oppose you' (Exodus 23:22). The New Testament places a high value on obedience, and every saint in every age has striven before all else to say without reservation, 'Not my will, but thine, be done!' Mere acts of obedience, a perfunctory going here and there at his direction, would denote bondage rather than obedience, and would not please God. Perfect obedience is of the Spirit, and includes love and willingness. Perfect obedience is only found where there is harmony with God.

In seeking to cultivate the spirit of obedience, leaders should be quick to detect the opposite spirit, that of opposition to authority. This spirit of opposition, even though exhibited in a very small matter, may indicate that the learner has not understood the importance of obedience, that he has not come to that state of mind that would mean willingness to set aside his own wishes.

When you detect that spirit of opposition in learners, take pains patiently to show them that resentment against authority, even in what may seem a very unimportant matter, may be as a little seed that will father a whole crop of tares. It is most important to teach the learner that the spirit of resentment, exposed in small matters now, is likely, unless conquered at once, to reappear later in a matter of life and death. Teach them that true obedience is of the spirit, and that they should obey instructions, even in seemingly unimportant matters, in the right spirit.

To establish a willing obedience in the learners is a very important part of your responsibility. The government of The Salvation Army is not a government of coercion. The highest form of government involves innate power to secure willing obedience, and this power has been ours in a unique degree. God bless you!

Reading Guide

Florence Booth continues laying a foundation for leader training by outlining the desired ethos of The Salvation Army system, including dynamics of sincerity, justice and obedience. Now, sincerity is an outworking of holiness. And holiness is known to solve most of life's problems. So if we got everyone sanctified we probably wouldn't need the rest of this book.

Remember, Florence Booth is not talking about justice in the sense of social justice issues with which we grapple today. She is dealing with justice in its basic sense, in terms of relationships within the training system. It may come across as naïve to many readers. However, she is writing in the context of The Salvation Army tackling several social injustices the world over. It may be that her concern for micro-justice helps to provide an environment in which the macro-injustices can be confronted effectively. Didn't Jesus teach that if we were faithful in small things we could be entrusted with much? It seemed to work with certain servants who had varied talents.

Then Florence Booth moves to the unpopular topic of obedience. If we were starting this book from scratch, this would certainly not top the list of dynamics we attempted to develop in creating an ethos for leader training! 'Obedience to properly constituted authority is the foundation of all moral excellence', said Catherine Booth. That is fine in regard to ethics. There will likely be few arguments there. But Florence Booth takes it further when she testifies:

Looking back over 44 years of officership, it seems to me impossible to speak too highly of the value and importance of Salvation Army discipline. During nearly six years of work as BC I realised very clearly that if all leaders had a truer idea, a stricter ideal, of obedience to rules and regulations, a much greater advance would be made throughout the Army world.

This is a massive statement. And it is not without merit. It has been a soapbox of some recently that obedience to *O&R* has not been tried and found wanting but found 'irrelevant' and 'obsolete' and not tried. Everything else under the sun has been tried, and you can see for yourself corps in your division slavishly imitating the Baptists, Pentecostals, and Anglicans. Most of those methods don't work very well when clothed in Salvationism.

However, all *O&R* are crafted to produce success in the salvation war. We are thoroughly convinced that conscientious application of *O&R* (for soldiers, local officers, corps officers and officers generally) can significantly advance the salvation war on your front.

Discussion Starters

1. How does holiness look in terms of sincerity?
2. How can holiness be propagated rather than merely sincerity?
3. How does the call for obedience sound in your context? Is it desirable? If so, how do you cultivate it?
4. How can we develop a more disciplined Army?
5. How might you reintroduce to soldiers, local officers and officers *O&R* in your leader training and on your local front?

[97] *Training Staff Council Lectures 1925*, 'The Spirit which should Possess the Training Work', 55, IHQ, 1925.
[98] It is my desire to speak to you of the spirit which should possess the Training Workers and pervade the Training Garrisons. There seems to be no one word that adequately represents that of which I am thinking; and yet I fancy you know what I mean by spirit.
[99] …peculiar…
[100] *This is a paraphrase of a complicated section of old-fashioned language.*
[101] *We return here to Mrs Booth's original text.*
[102] …labour…
[103] …it cannot truly be said that any Training Staff or Garrison is possessed and governed by this spirit unless this spirit dominates each class, each Field Meeting, each interview, and finds expression in every arrangement and decision belonging to the work.
[104] *A large section of original text is omitted here, comparing the influence of Salvation Army leader training with that of home life on an individual.*
[105] …Alas…
[106] *Benevolence is part of the spirit which should possess the Training Work.* [This sentence was italicised in the original.] If true benevolence prevails, the Cadets (even those who must be sent away) will feel that their own highest good is sought as well as the highest good of The Army to which they belong.
[107] The Training Garrison cannot but be a hotbed of religion.
[108] *A large section about the need for sincerity in prayer is omitted here.*
[109] A knowledge that God desires sincerity before all else in His children, and a horror of falling short of sincerity, is one of the essential features of the experience of holiness.
[110] …but rather to seek after those who, as to cleverness, gifts, and graces, may appear backward and halting, and yet are true gold in their uttermost sincerity and conscientiousness. It is for Officers to seek after such, to see that they are encouraged and that their quality is duly appreciated.
[111] What a source of suffering is the lack of justice in the world at large!…Beginning in the bosom of the family, and then looking out on to the wide world…
[112] …mar your work as a whole…
[113] *Another fault which easily obtrudes itself and is equally destructive of justice is prejudice.* [This was italicised in the original.]
[114] *A long section of detailed advice is omitted here.*
[115] *This paragraph is abridged and paraphrased.*

Chapter 5
We Believe in Miracles: Development of Character[116]
by Lieut-Colonel Catherine Bramwell-Booth
International Training Staff Council 1925

The training leader must be convinced that character is prone to improvement by the Holy Spirit.[117]

WE believe in miracles! We should be no good as trainers if we did not; and we must see that leaders under our direction are also confirmed in this faith – that it is possible to develop character. Character is not soul. It is not mind. Some of the cleverest people have but poor character. It is not will. Some strong-willed people have thoroughly bad characters. What is it? I do not know.

It seems to me that character is something we cannot quite explain. As a training leader, I have sometimes felt I would rather have a learner who is inferior in gifts yet possessing real character, than one who is capable, but weak in character. If your people have character, you are likely to accomplish more with them in the end than with the brilliant people who lack in this something we are talking about.

One of our leading officers told me he was once on a long railway journey with one other gentleman in the carriage. He soon began to talk of the Army and its work, and this man said, 'I'm sorry, but I do not believe as you do. When one comes to enter the fields of science one is obliged to abandon much that one believed in before. I do not say there is no God, but I cannot believe there is any Power that is interfering with the development of the human race today. I think we are left to get on as best we can. There may be a Power somewhere, but, if so, I do not know where. Everything is under fixed laws, you cannot change a man, or a dog!'

My comrade (he was a colonel) turned to him and said, 'If you knew The Salvation Army you could not think that. We must believe because we see bad men changed. How would you account for that?'

The man replied, 'As a matter of fact, my dear sir, it does not happen; you think they are bad, but they are not really bad; or you think they are good, and they are not really good. Nothing is really changed! It is all according to the shape of the brain. Take yourself, for example, I can see what you are when I look into your face. I am a phrenologist.'

Then the colonel said, 'Be honest, I have been honest with you. Feel my bumps and see just what I am. What do you really think I should be?'

The phrenologist felt his head. He was absolutely nonplussed and said, 'I must admit if I judged merely from this I should not expect to find you in any way connected with religion. You lack veneration; I must say you are a most interesting case,' and he began to question him about how long he had been in The Salvation Army. I suppose he was trying to find out whether the colonel was one of the good ones, or one who only seemed to be good.

This incident impressed me at the time (I was on training work) because it confirmed much that I liked to think – for instance, that our natural limitations have very little to do with what God can make of us if we really give ourselves up to him. To remember that, and to teach the learners that, is especially helpful in these days, when the very people we are trying to help are often tainted with psychological nonsense.[118]

There is a lot of talk today about a person's natural tendencies. We are told a child's bent must not be changed, he must be allowed to do everything he wants to do, even to falling in the fire! I do not know quite how far they go. Some of the learners have picked up a bit of it. They say, 'Well, of course, that is not my gifting,'[119] or 'This is my make up,' or 'Yes, I know it's a failing but my father was like it, it's in our family,' and settle down to be content with what they are. We have to introduce them to the great fact, new to them, that God can change them.

I was inexperienced when suddenly planted down, a cadet among a crowd of others. I had not been to school, nor mixed with many people. There had been enough of us at home to make ideal companionships within our own circle, and when I was suddenly plunged into the midst of a crowd, I was depressed at my own limitations, and I thought, I will never be able to be and do what I ought to be and want to do, and what the war requires.[120]

Dear Commissioner Rees helped me. I do not think he ever lectured on any subject without bringing in at the beginning, or at the end, 'Well, remember! *What you are not by nature you can be by grace.*' Do you believe it? He simply drilled this into us. We were always hearing it; and could not get away from it. He used to say it to us again and again, and it has remained with me: 'What you are not by nature you can be by grace.'

That was of inestimable value to us as cadets. We felt that whatever our limitations, we can rise above them. That is how training leaders ought to make the learners feel. We believe God can change people,[121] and this being so we should strive with all our might to create in the minds of the learners a living faith in the possibility of their own development. Keep on saying to them as the Lord said when one came to him in perplexity: '"If you can?" said Jesus. "Everything is possible for one who believes"' (Mark 9:23).

Further, if we are convinced that character is a matter for development, and are striving to create in the minds of the learners a living faith for their own development, *we shall guard every evidence of growth*. Sometimes evidences of growth of character are expressed very clumsily. A learner may strike out and do a new thing, but do it altogether badly. Training leaders must be wise enough and quick enough to see behind that lack of skill, for frequently they will find a motive, an impulse which is really a most encouraging sign of development in that character. Guard carefully against any desire to correct an error, if your correction might at the same time injure a blessed impulse of growth.

In training plants, the first years count so much. For instance, if trees are going to live and develop, it is amazing how much depends on guarding them during the first years. If the main shoot is broken when the tree is only a few inches high, the tree will be deformed. For hundreds of years, maybe, it will live and try to correct that deformity, but it will never be perfect, never be the same again.

You can go through any forest and see trees which have been injured in their youth. It is sometimes like that with character: some stultifying influence is brought to bear on it, and that which should have developed into beauty is injured, hurt or shrinks away, and that soul is maimed.

It is very strange how people persist in the colossal error that it is much easier to deal with a person's spiritual nature than with their physical nature. The most delicate and rare skill is required from those who seek to help in the development of character. This is especially so for leaders engaged in training. Of course, skill is needed in all our dealings with souls, but especially in training, where we have them in our care day after day. The younger leaders coming up in training work need to be helped by you to consider it so that they may approach their work with care and preparation, and be guarded from making mistakes. It has been disappointing to find how blunderingly and haphazardly many are prepared to rush in and deal with a soul.

We must maintain our faith for those for whom we are working. It is not enough to begin with faith. A physician says, 'While there is life there is hope.' And I think the training leader should feel, 'While they are learners there is hope.' At any rate, it is important that the learner should feel that. I have seen an almost blighting effect produced on souls because they have felt a leader had no faith in them. The learners, whatever their own discouragements, down-heartedness and failures may be, should each be able to say, 'My training leaders have faith for me.'

The training leader must believe the development of character may be assisted by human instrumentality

We must not only believe, and make the learners believe, that God can change them, we must also believe God will use us to help bring about that change. The steadfast faith of one heart for another may exercise an immeasurable influence. I do not think we have learned to understand that fully yet. It is one of the mysteries of the spiritual world to me, one of the things I wish I saw more clearly.

When I have stopped to think and pray about it, as I have done, I have been frightened. It has made my inner soul tremble, especially when I have come up to interviews, and have been faced with the thought that perhaps what I say in this next hour may really make a difference to that soul, to its development, to its future. It is tremendous! We cannot get away from it; it is happening all the time; we must accept it as we have accepted so much in God's plan which we do not understand.

Speaking for myself, at any rate, I do not understand it. I can only say it is so, and I must accept it. We cannot doubt it, because we have evidence that this is his way of working amongst us, and we have evidence of it in our own experience. I certainly have in mine. I look back to people, this one, and that one, and thank God that they ever touched my spirit: they gave me something, did something for me, and made me different from what I should have been if I had not come in touch with them. I am bound to say I cannot doubt that human beings help to mould each other because my own life and heart would contradict such a doubt.

There are many ways of assisting in the development of the character of those entrusted to our care. *We should do all we can to inspire them. Hold up an ideal before them until it becomes a thing they desire, something for which their own hearts reach out with longing.*

Desire! Oh, if we could only get it really burning in their hearts! Then we could almost fold our hands and let the Holy Spirit and the soul go their way, for that soul's development would be assured. We have a part in the kindling, the stirring up, the creating of desire. If desire for spiritual light, life and love be strong enough, that desire is to be fulfilled. This is the Lord's promise: 'Whatever you ask for in prayer, believe that you have received it, and it will be yours' (Mark 11:24).

We may assist in the development of character by inculcating the laws that belong to growth. Do not be afraid of repetition. When I was in the training garrison I was greatly impressed by going through the gospels and noticing for myself all the occasions on which it is clearly stated, or implied, that the Lord said the same thing over again, or did the same thing over again.

'And as was his custom, he taught them' (Mark 10:1). And then how often the parables came back to the same lesson! This encouraged my own heart and made me feel, 'No matter how often I have to go over essentials, I will go over them until I feel they are really in the learners' minds.' This repetition is necessary to the inculcating of the laws of character. We cannot too often insist upon such foundation laws of progress as:

Sincerity

A person's character cannot be developed for good if they are not sincere, no matter what you do for them, or they do for themselves, or how splendid may be all the machinery for helping them. For the development of character in the right direction, sincerity is absolutely essential; and natural gifts have nothing to do with this. Help the learners to get away from themselves, and make them understand sincerity.

Some, alas, do not understand what it is to have a true heart. It is a difficult matter to deal with; but sincerity is essential to any soul aspiring to progress in the way of God. Deal with it from every aspect, so that, whether they accept the law for themselves or not, no learners can be in doubt as to the meaning and importance of sincerity.

Perseverance

We must make plain, by continual repetition if necessary, the part which perseverance plays in progress. It is wonderful how often the natural laws are a tangible representation of the spiritual. Personally I believe this is part of God's plan to enlighten us, that we may know him, his nature and his will for us, to a marvellous extent by studying his work. I think this is written large over God's creation – if we want to attain, it is decreed that we must do it by perseverance in work.

Here again Commissioner Rees helped me. There were two things he emphasised. One, 'What you are not by nature you can be by grace', the other (and I think he used to bring it in somehow every day), 'You must work!' In his illustrations, talks and lectures, he would say: 'You are no good if you cannot work. My dear boy, if you cannot work, you had better clear out!'

He emphasised it so much that he almost made us feel it didn't matter what work we did so long as we worked. He used to tell us about his weaknesses and shortcomings, and then add, 'But I worked! I got up early in the morning and I went to work. I had to work when I was a cadet; I had to work when I was a lieutenant; and now I am a commissioner I work! If you do not want to work you will not get anywhere.' He rubbed it in with all his might. Perhaps some of us worked too hard; but I think it was erring on the right side.

The mastery of self

I am but mentioning a few foundation laws necessary to the development of character. *No high development of a person in any direction, spiritual, mental, or physical, is possible without a governing of themself and their faculties.* The person who sets out to be an acrobat has to govern their body, and master those physical powers which are theirs, that they may excel. They have to exercise their muscles until they are under such perfect control that each is brought into submission.

In a similar way, someone[122] who wants to excel in the field of mental activity has to subdue their thoughts that they may properly use their mind. Equally, a person of character must be master of their impulses.

We must help the learners in the development of character by giving them *room to exercise the qualities we are seeking to develop*. In this connection you must not ignore nor despise small things. Ordinary humdrum experiences may be used for the development of the highest and rarest gifts. The spirit of unselfishness can be truly exhibited in an ordinary rough-and-tumble day as much as in the moment when a person lays down their life for another. We must make the learners realise this and help them to exercise the qualities of which we speak to them, and towards which they are reaching out. *Let us use their relationships with each other to help them.* A learner who is selfish and disagreeable amongst comrades will act selfishly in their duties to souls. A selfish person will not willingly carry the burden in the work of God; they may come in for the glory where they can, but will be likely to shirk the burden and shirk the work.

The leaders should make their people feel that the qualities they need as leaders may be exercised at the learners' meal table and in the dormitory and on the march, and in the corps, just as much as anywhere else.

We should also use the learners' attitude toward their leaders. If you want a person to develop in a right spirit, and in the character which is going to make them the person we want in the future, let them show those qualities as a learner towards their superiors. People who resent being told things, what a nuisance they are! They must be approached so carefully, and the moment they are corrected they are all bristly and upset. That sort of spirit ought to be dealt with in the learners; they must have opportunity for exercising the right kind of spirit towards their leaders.

Then learners should have opportunity to exercise themselves in voluntary works and discipline. I perhaps feel more strongly on this than many feel. I hope I did not make a mistake, but I set a high value on what the learner did of his own accord, and I think we should make more opportunity for voluntary work. There is a tendency in that direction here… We do not decide so much as formerly what learners shall do in their field work and in the meetings. We leave the door open so that we may know those whose own hearts push them to action. When, without being actually called upon, they are drawn out in testimony, we find the people who have it in them – it is the voluntary testimony that is valuable.

I feel also that we ought to give the learners ample opportunity for *voluntary works of self-discipline.* I found it helped me considerably, and I know it has helped scores of others I have come into contact with, *to impose some yoke on themselves.* Apart altogether from the value of what they do, this self-discipline does something for their own character.

I have said sometimes to learners, 'Will you for the next month, whatever happens, whatever you feel, get up one half-hour earlier to read and pray and study?' I have proved that, apart from the benefit derived from the study (I do not say the reading and study does not do good, I am sure it does), that grip on themselves, that *making themselves do it,* adds something to character which is of infinite value. The Bible says, 'It is good for a man to bear the yoke while he is young' (Lamentations 3:27). Well, I think by putting a yoke on himself in his youth he has certainly gone a long way towards being a man fit to impose a yoke on others.

There should be opportunity for the learner to do more than is expected of him. God save us and protect us from leaders who cannot do more than they are supposed to do! Why, the Army would never be what it is, we should never be sitting here, if our leaders and comrades and the saints who have gone before us had not done more than anyone expected them to do! In the past they did not wait to know whether this particular department was supposed to do this or that. The need imposed the responsibility to meet it if possible.

One of our failures in the development of our present-day young people and leaders is that, in spite of all we do, we turn out too many who are merely prepared to go through the daily task: so many hours visiting, and so much time for this and that; leaders who say: 'What things I am supposed to do I have done, I am a faithful servant,' and go to bed in peace!

This is not enough! When you think of the countries where our leaders are working, do you think it is enough? It is not enough! The Salvation Army needs people who, when they have done all that is required of them, will still say, 'I am an unworthy servant. What more can I do?'

Let us give the learners room to exercise this spirit while in training. If every moment of the day is taken up and it takes the whole of their strength to do what they are supposed to do (and you must have mercy on the limitations of human strength), then with the best will in the world they cannot do more than they are expected to do. Let us, whilst still telling them to go so far, see that they shall always have strength – if they have the heart – to go farther.

In this matter, and indeed in all that has to do with the development of character, the small training programmes have an immense advantage over the larger. I know that in the smaller programmes you have fewer leaders; but the smaller your company, the finer your opportunity to make people of character.

Leaders should be one with you. And let me say in passing, teach our young leaders to let the learners help themselves. It is an old-fashioned difficulty. It is far easier to do things for people than to leave them to do things for themselves, and one of the snares of training work is that very often the love, zeal, faith and desire in the hearts of the leaders push them on to do for the learners what the learners ought to be left to do for themselves; and we must teach the younger leaders that part of the skill they must acquire in dealing with souls is not only to know *when* to help, but also when *not* to help; the one needs quite as able a mind and heart as the other.

We may assist in their development by helping the learners to find out for themselves about themselves. After all, it is only what a person does for themself that can develop them, and that is why it is so important to encourage voluntary effort on the part of the learner even in the simplest things, in their public work, and in the use of their time. It is what they do for themselves that will help them. Learners must be helped to know themselves and find out what is in them, and then helped to deal with their weaknesses, if their character is to develop as we desire.

The learners must be armed against dangers in themselves. Are there any other dangers? I do not know whether you agree with me, but I am tempted to say that there are no dangers really worth calling dangers to a person's soul and spirit apart from the danger which exists in themself. My experience in dealing with learners individually led me to feel this, and the longer I was at it the more firmly I became convinced of the falsity of the argument that environment makes the person. The exceptions were too many.

I have met some who are strong in the belief that environment has a great deal to do with character. I must say I think that if training leaders would take trouble to look behind the scenes they would come to the conclusion that environment has very little to do with deciding a person's character. I have studied the learners from this standpoint and, in the majority of cases, I have been compelled to the conclusion that environment has had quite a different effect from what I should have expected.

Failures, in my opinion, are caused by the inherent weaknesses in a person's character rather than by his circumstances, and these weaknesses are what we should teach the learners to discover in themselves. All have some weaknesses. The strongest character has its weakness. No one is without a weak spot in character, and we must show the learners that *their very strength often involves weakness.*

Take, for example, the will, one of the finest assets in character building. We say that strong-willed people are the people to make leaders; and it is true that a strong will *is* an asset towards making a fine character. But we have all had experience, also, of how a strong will can cause havoc and disaster. When strong will remains self-will, the strong-willed person becomes one of the most heartbreaking of all. When we have to deal with him we look at what good we saw in him, the capacity and the promise, and we see how because of self-will his whole life has turned to failure.[123] His strength was also his weakness.

I do not think it hurts the learners to tell them we think God has given them this or that quality and to mention their good qualities. The learner is sometimes tremendously astonished, had never thought there was anything good about that tendency, and when you sit down and tell him that you feel he is gifted it helps him to a certain self-respect which is good for human nature. Then you can go on to show him how to turn these gifts to good account and to warn him how they may become a danger.

Show the learners also that they must deal with failure in themselves, and that weakness and failure left uncorrected will ruin the finest character. If you are going to show the learners how to build a good character, you cannot allow them to tolerate weaknesses and little failures side by side with strength. Failures and weaknesses must be mastered, corrected, turned out if necessary and, if possible, lost. Many weaknesses cannot altogether be banished; they remain and have to be mastered.

Teach them, further, that all gifts and talents should be servants. Help the learner to deal with himself by showing him that his gifts and talents ought to be his servants, and that servants must not rule the master. If you can make him understand this it will help him. Show him how the gifts God has given can be rightly used.

As an illustration, take the gift of quick judgement. I do not know whether you have much trouble with your young people, but in our country we sometimes have difficulty because of their quickness to judge and criticise; at any rate, I found this a difficulty, and because of it many learners close the door to blessing.

It is not exactly cynicism, but a certain fashion of picking holes, finding fault, turning up their noses at this and that and the other. Sometimes it does an immense amount of harm, especially when people influence each other. I have found it a help to some of them when I have said, 'I notice you are rather critical.' Generally these people are proud of their critical minds, and they have replied, 'Perhaps I am,' expecting me to condemn them. But, instead of that, I have often said, 'Have you thanked God for this gift?'

'No, not exactly!' 'Well, it is a gift – a great gift. If you are thinking of being a leader of men, that discernment and clear mind which enables you to judge quickly ranks, perhaps, as one of the highest qualities you will need in order to be a good leader.' Then I have talked about the abuse of the critical faculty: how some who have this faculty have let it run away with them so that they cannot go to a meeting without being led away from the subject of the meeting to criticise this and that. I have tried to show that this is the master in bondage to the servant, and that the spirit of criticism which has, perhaps, often led them into condemnation, can be so governed, mastered, and trained as to be one of the greatest help to them.

Then I think you should help the learners to believe that all weakness can be made a means of grace. I hope that is not putting it too strongly. I think God's dealings and records in the Bible give us a right to say that, when it is not the Lord's will to take away a weakness, he will make it a means of grace.

I have known people absolutely under bondage through fear of other people, and have seen that weakness taken right away; but sometimes a soul will pray not only three times, as Paul prayed, but far more often, and yet a particular weakness is not removed, because it is God's purpose to let it remain; but, with a recognition of his will, there comes a promise: 'My grace is sufficient for you, for my power is made perfect in weakness' (2 Corinthians 12:9). We want to make the learners understand that if they have a weakness which it seems part of God's will shall remain, they can bless God because that weakness in them is going to be, throughout their future, a means of grace: something that will make them better because it will keep them in close touch with God, or keep them more humble, or more tender.

Every learner should be convinced that development is essential to spiritual health. Root and ground them in this belief: salvation and sanctification are the preparation for development, just as the preparing of the ground and the putting in of the seed are the first steps towards a bringing forth of fruit.

Spiritual growth is a sign of holiness. Holiness has been called spiritual health. 'Where there is growth, there is life' – this is very clearly one of God's messages to us in the natural world, where I think we can say growth and life are almost synonymous terms. I have often asked myself, is not the fact that we keep on growing one of the inward, silent tokens of immortality? I am growing older, but the older I am, the more I see how many things I have to learn, and how much there is I wish I knew. My desire to know is getting stronger and stronger. May I not conclude that this is one of God's silent whispers to me, telling me that he has much to do for me yet, and that this little life is a mere nothing, so far as its capacity to satisfy my spirit is concerned. But this is in passing. Let the learners understand they must go on developing.

It is a heartbreaking truth that leaders backslide! Some I have had to deal with in bitter anguish of spirit. The awfulness of seeing people who have walked with God, tasted the joys of the Spirit, engaged in the service for souls and won other souls, turned back into sin – even into gross sin! I have said to myself: 'Why is it? How can this thing be? How can it be?' Doesn't it sometimes come to you as a blow? It has to me. Perhaps I have not seen the comrades concerned in the interval, and have suddenly heard of some awful thing happening, some black cloud having descended, and they have gone out of sight. I have felt if only I could speak to them and say, 'I cannot believe it. It cannot be *you*! You could not have done that, not the *you* I knew – how could you?' Alas, for the dull answer of fact!

Sometimes I have looked at the learners when they have come near to commissioning, during the crowded days before they must go marching out; looked at them and felt that they were learners for the last time. I have said to myself, 'I shall never have the right in the same way to take them aside and say, heart to heart and face-to-face, what I want to say, and what God gives me to say.'

Looking at them as a body for the last time, I have asked myself, 'Who among them shall be lost? Who?' As I have looked into their faces I have felt it cannot be that one, or this one; and, looking at them one after another, I have been unable to think it of any. And yet I always knew (and you always know) that within so many years there will be empty places.

I do not mean the blanks caused by sickness, or death, or circumstances which may turn people away but which they cannot control. I mean those blanks which come because of souls stepping back into sin and wrongdoing.

Why is it? Why is it? God's will is higher than our will. If we would keep them in the way of purity, holiness, and right-doing, how much more would their Heavenly Father keep them in his way. Why do they step out of the way?

I think one of the reasons is that they have not really grasped this truth of God's law, which cannot and will not change, that if they do not grow, if their spiritual life does not develop, if their character is not getting better, they are in that place of danger where at any moment the tempter may step in and destroy them. They are like the tree that, ceasing to grow, begins to rot; when the wind blows, down it comes. But the rotting, the period of cessation of growth, had begun weeks or months, if not years, before the storm, before the crash.

Let us warn the young leaders we send out, of the perils of the way. Let us get them to carry this lesson with them: I must advance. If I stop growing I shall come to grief. So God will build up characters that will be like him. 'What we will be has not yet been made known. But we know that when Christ appears, we shall be like him, for we shall see him as he is' (1 John 3:2). May it be so with these souls he has given us!

Reading Guide

Catherine Bramwell-Booth presses hard on what we might, today, call spiritual disciplines, accessed by means of grace. While popular in some circles, the terminology hasn't seeped into Salvation Army culture significantly. Sure, some people fast, a few undergo solitude and others practise other spiritual disciplines. But we do partake of the means of grace in different ways. For example, 24-7 prayer is a massive Salvation Army endeavour, with more than 500 non-stop prayer rooms set up around the world. In many places we gather for holiness meetings as well as knee-drill, open-air meetings, soldiers' meetings, Bible studies and cell groups. Understood from the perspective of means of grace, these exercises provide intentional and regular opportunity for development of character.

One of the messages emerging from her teaching is the importance of being ruthless with our schedules. Character can be improved both by the Holy Spirit and human instrumentality. Discipline and interaction with the means of grace are the channel to that improvement. It is through such engagement that the Holy Spirit often operates. And it exposes us to teaching and rigours from a human standpoint that strengthen character and position us to lead from a solid base.

Catherine Bramwell-Booth argues that learners must go on developing. Lifelong learning is what we might call it today. And as the responsibilities change and increase it is important that our character and capacity grow similarly. As Christian author and speaker Joyce Meyer said, 'new levels, new devils'. The spiritual response ought to be 'higher appointing, higher anointing'. Leader training cannot be something we simply tick off on a 'to-do' list along with reading certain books and attending certain conferences.

Discussion Starters

1. How do you intentionally develop character in yourself? In your learners?
2. Have you a plan for development of your character with

relation to your leadership abilities and tasks? How does/might it look?

3. 'Spiritual growth is a sign of holiness' – discuss this statement and the flip side – lack of spiritual growth a sign of lack of holiness.

---

[116] *Training Staff Council Lectures 1925*, 'Development of Character', 109, IHQ, 1925.
[117] The Training Officer must be convinced that character is a matter for development, and that alteration in a man for the better is the work of the Holy Spirit.
[118] …bosh…
[119] …bent…
[120] …I shall never rise up to be what I ought to be and want to be, and what the Work requires.
[121] …men… *[from here on, what was 'men' in the original text, is now generally changed to 'people'].*
[122] In like manner a man…
[123] …gone to smash.

Chapter 6
Training Character
outline notes of General Albert Orsborn's lecture
International Training Staff Council 1951

I THINK I would say we have laboured in vain if we fail in training to do some real testing, proving, correcting, balancing and strengthening of the learner's character. We do not mean characteristics in the sense of distinctive or peculiar marks of individuality – a loud voice, a confident swagger, a smile, a laugh. Normally we mean personality, something distinctive, out of the ordinary, definite lines, notable.

There are some such learners – not too many – in every session. Value them! Don't try to standardise them, they are precious, if at times inconvenient to authority. But nowadays 'personality' is a word widely used, about all kinds of animate and inanimate objects: houses, dogs, birds, hats, suits, pictures. We must go deeper to know what we mean by a learner's character.

'Character' means something engraved: impressions, marks in a person's way of thinking and acting. These marks may be family traits, or the evidence of hard or easy circumstances: the way people have acted towards him; the record of his own protracted habits. Other meanings: temperament, temper, reputation, disposition. Though difficult to define, it is similar to the art critic who said (snapping his fingers): 'It lacks that!'

We do not mean soul, at least not altogether, though the character we are after is powerfully influenced by the soul. Mind, yes, but not the intellect. [There are] Many clever, gifted, but quite ineffective people. 'A man may hang upon his name the whole haberdashery of success, yet go to his grave a failure.' But since the mind of a man is the spring of his actions, character must be something to do with it.

Will – obviously weak-willed people lack character. Some strong-willed people also. Of course the will has a great deal to do with making and keeping character. Character is the total personality, wrought into being by thought and action. It has its roots in conduct and it is powerfully influenced by small beginnings. Character is seldom fixed or static. It is living and is commensurate with life itself.

Character is training priority number one

The reception, expression, retention of religious truth depends on the reliability of character. We teach that God can use anyone. That is true within reasonable limits, short of mental or physical deficiency. But we must not convey the idea there is nothing for the subject to do except surrender.

'Thou art the potter, I am the clay' is only one side of the truth. God gives us seeds; we grow our own flowers. 'God is never in the ready-made business.'

God will not entrust his greatest gifts to unreliable people: people who are too indolent or ignorant or selfish to acknowledge and correct their faults. He is 'no respecter of persons', but he certainly is of character and fitness.

That the Holy Spirit is fire is true; but he is fire shot through and through with principle.

As the lamp to the current, the camera to the picture, the instrument to the player, so is character the means, the medium whose defects or preparedness influence even the extent of usefulness to God. Remember we are training for leadership even though some will always be assistants. We must be discerners: seers. Discern between present state and possibilities. Do not let weak or wrong character slip through. We can best afford their loss. We shall never get more leaders by commissioning nonentities.

Our training system exists by and for the learner

Whether he knows it is a moot point, but we do. We invest a lot in each one. He costs a lot (average about £200 [equivalent to approximately

£5,000 in 2012] here). And some say, 'He's not worth it.' Do you know any form of cultivation that is all profit?

We do not set the routine, the rules, the timetable above the learner. There are times when the unusual must be done; the machinery is second to the man or woman.

Order and tidiness, these are very lovely, but they are not the be-all and end-all of existence. And not by any means are they as important to character as some would have us believe. Don't whistle and use artificial aids. Don't be touchy about the institution and for ever judging its value.

Over some programmes one could write:
Dusters and timetables,
Whistles and rectangles:
These be thy gods, O Israel!

Training is not a series of straight lines, rules and cubes…it is individual, adaptable; it is not hamstrung by its own organisation. We must not make training easy. Nothing is so vicious as to leave a learner unchallenged. We must extend him. We must avoid the dulling effect of routine; beware of giving learners a feeling that any part of training is futile and useless.

Training system: the season of new beginnings

Some have never really had character tested. 'Frailest where I seem the best, only strong for lack of test.' Creatures of heredity, environment, convention.

Sincerity of their call is proved by willingness to accept a new outlook and undergo structural alterations.

Unlearn first.

Emotional content of religion [is] valuable but also dangerous. A strong engine in a faulty car or boat is dangerous.

Get the learner to believe he is not obliged to accept himself as he is.

Changing means development, not artificiality. Refusal to change is [a person's] own death sentence – the coarse-grained man need not remain so because his family is so; the refined, quiet girl does not become untrue to herself by coming out of herself. 'Good' is not always 'good enough' and 'do well' has always been the enemy of 'do better'.

There is a lot of damaging talk about determination: learners say [it's] 'not my nature'.

Impress [upon] the learner [that] the most important training leader is himself. Overseers, teachers, [are] important. [They] Can give light, make suggestions, expose failures, even create desire. The actual grappling and growth are entirely *personal*!

Learners must be taught to stand up to their difficulties. Avoidance is a line of least resistance[,] fatal to character – Satan is now drawn as a curve: the line of least resistance.

Our work [is] indivisible from unfavourable reactions, unwillingness, opposition, differences of principle.

Only by facing and conquering your difficulty, or at least your fear of it, will your character be formed. Learners must be taught to start on this at once.

Tackling difficulties: personal, official, external, internal, circumstantial, sequential, incidental.

We do well to remember that character-making is not the mere correction of faults. We need trainers, not microscopic critics. Sharp critics tend to be poor judges. Watch for the praiseworthy. Encourage the good.

A few important elements

The importance of detailed observation. Nothing is insignificant. An incident, word, look, taken alone, may appear unimportant. Association with other things may, probably will, make a composite picture. Therefore we use small things.

Does not youthful character develop from the way a job is done, a bed made, a book read, a duty performed? And of course the learner's own standards in these things.

That is why we observe: the learners' rooms; punctuality without assistance; work sections, wash-up; behaviour, manners; walking or sitting; honesty in study and in preparation; proper respect for authority. This training is built on detail. These leaders have to represent the Army; we need character in them.

A comment on the Founder's attitude on early-day Army marriages:

But an unexpected, though substantial, difficulty appeared in the way of fulfilling this wish: the women who joined the Army were generally better-bred and of a gentler nature than the men; and it was not easy, even for devout and selfless women, to live in the intimacy of marriage with men whose manners were extraordinarily rough and ready. Booth had said that he would obtain his soldiers from the public houses, and many of them were reclaimed drunkards. It is one thing, however, to reclaim a drunkard, and another thing to reform his table manners if those have been elementary. A man may realise the iniquity of habitual drunkenness without realising that there is anything wrong in a gross way of feeding. Booth, who was sensitive as a woman about such matters, quickly perceived that if Army marriages were to be successful, the comparatively trifling matter of the right use of knives and forks and the discipline of bodily gases should receive attention. He had to teach some of his soldiers the laws of decent behaviour at dinner!

Their strong points may conceal weaknesses

Tell him his good points: wise and encouraging. But show him how virtues may become faults.

- Willpower may become obstinacy.
- Self-respect may become pride.
- Emotion may become laxity.
- Criticism may become cynicism.
- Courage may become rashness.
- Candour may become rudeness.
- Silence may become secretiveness.

Teach them the necessity for hard and unremitting toil

Time-servers never made and cannot maintain the Army. Trade union ideas of hours and wages are entirely foreign to us. The leader must be one whose work is a master thought. Look for opportunities to teach the learner personal restraint – humility. (A grace specially protected against imitation.)

Sincerity…the most valuable ingredient of character.

Truth…is an absolute applied only to Christ: 'I am… the truth' (John 14:6). But the principle of truth must be applied in character. Not always saying all you know to be true; but keeping truth in all you say. Sometimes remembering silence can be false. Be extremely careful how you condemn something or someone as untrue. There are infinite gradations of truth and falsehood. Intention is the important thing.

Obedience…some show an arrogant spirit; in bearing, in demeanour, in attitude, in sarcasm and roughness. They demonstrate an unwillingness to obey, especially where the direction comes from a peer, or newer leader. Obsequiousness towards superiors often goes with it. [Leaders] Must be quick to detect and correct this spirit.

Application…the influence of the training leader.

Everything we desire to create in the learner must first be in us. That is the nature of our training – we rely on the character and spirituality of the training leaders. Learners are quick to judge this.

The training leader must hide his own superiority. His business is not to win admiration, but to act like light on the opening flowers.

The training leader must never show resentment. Never show personal resentment or anger towards a learner's mistakes, indiscretions, even misdeeds that are of the very stuff of training. I question the efficiency of any training system where life proceeds placidly and the leaders are seldom engaged in difficult personal correction, rebuke, and training of the individual learner. But never must the leader show that he is offended, insulted, or annoyed; his must be the restraint and patience of love.

Training leaders must be approachable, even lovable. Do not repel the offering of a learner's appreciation and affection. It is an important thing to give encouragement to the power of love – and I am not thinking of sexual attraction, but of the power in one personality to call out and develop the best in another.

First, 'Do not repel.' Then, 'Win and retain learner's confidence.' What you *are* is of paramount importance. You must give the impression of being a leader who cares profoundly for the individual. Learners will remember and profit – as we did – by personal influence. Indeed… character-making is as individual as all precious things are.

Reading Guide

General Orsborn was one of our most eloquent leaders. Our disappointment with this chapter is that all we have remaining from his lecture is the outline.

The complete text as he delivered it would have been much more clear and persuasive. However, the subject matter is important and his thoughts incisive.

It is worth highlighting accountability here. Accountability is an essential component of discipling relationships, and The Salvation Army has used covenant accountability effectively to advance training into leadership.

Albert Orsborn relentlessly prods into what seem, in some cases, fairly trivial aspects of life and comportment, convinced that they indicate flaws in character. To dig this hard into someone's life requires mutual respect and agreed accountability.

Accountability, when practised, has protected the salvation warfare of leaders throughout history. Its absence is like a huge target painted on a leader at which Satan and his minions can fire blasts until they hit the bullseye and, sadly, there is a scandal that knocks the leader out of action.

But we are not unaware of the devil's schemes. We know that he will attack leaders, often in the areas outlined in Richard Foster's book, *Money, Sex and Power*.[124]

The strongest protection is holiness. And an aid to that is accountability. This is not new teaching. The Salvation Army was born out of Methodism, famous for class meeting vulnerability and disciplined accountability.

The Army adapted these features, developing a ward system and a

A Field for Exploits

system for self-examination that, when applied, protects soldiers and leaders from the sin that so easily entangles.

Here is the test for self-examination. It is a great schedule to have your accountability partners ask you, and it also works powerfully when you ask God for the answers.

Test for Self-examination

The following are questions taken from The Salvation Army's *O&R for Soldiers*, titled *Chosen to be a Soldier*.[125]

1. Am I habitually guilty of any known sin? Do I practise or allow myself in any thought, word or deed which I know to be wrong?

2. Am I so the master of my bodily appetites as to have no condemnation? Do I allow myself in any indulgence that is injurious to my holiness, growth in knowledge, obedience or usefulness?

3. Are my thoughts and feelings such as I should not be ashamed to hear published before God?

4. Does the influence of the world cause me to do or say things that are unlike Christ?

5. Do my tempers cause me to act, or feel or say things that I see afterward are contrary to that love which I ought to bear always to those about me?

6. Am I doing all in my power for the salvation of sinners? Do I feel concern about their danger, and pray and work for their salvation as if they were my children?

7. Am I fulfilling the vows I have made to God in my acts of consecration, or at the penitent form?

8. Is my example in harmony with my profession ['profession' being an archaic term for 'testimony']?

9. Am I conscious of any pride or haughtiness in my manner or bearing?

10. Do I conform to the fashions and customs of the world, or do I show that I despise them?

11. Am I in danger of being carried away with worldly desire to be rich or admired?

Discussion Starters

1. Does General Orsborn overdo it? Where do you draw the line?

2. How can we replicate conditions today to accomplish the ends he describes? Is it desirable?

3. Are you in an accountability relationship? How can you draw your learners into such a process?

4. How can you ensure that this exercise encourages, edifies and avoids the inclination to devolve into microscopic criticism?

---

[124] Richard Foster, *Money, Sex and Power*, Hodder Christian Books, 1999.
[125] *Chosen To Be a Soldier - Orders and Regulations for Soldiers of The Salvation Army*, 17-18, IHQ, 1999.

Chapter 7
Profile of Leadership – the Training Principal, Today and Tomorrow
by General Erik Wickberg
International Training Principals' Conference 1974

IN Commissioner Karl Larsson's office there used to hang a text with some words by the great Norwegian explorer Fridtjof Nansen. In a somewhat free translation into English they said: 'When I reach the top of the mountain: I lift up my eyes to catch a glimpse of the next.'

In The Salvation Army, the institutionalised position responsible for training officer leaders is that of training principal, and it is a profile of this kind of leadership that I shall attempt. I am not so sure that my own training principal would be satisfied with this introduction, for it would, to him, sound too apologetic. He used to say to us: 'Don't apologise! Get on with it!'

What I intend to do is to draw your attention to a few essentials, which we look for and expect when a training principal is appointed. We feel we have a right to do this, for not only do we look for them – the cadets will look for them, comrade officers will look for them, and outsiders, friendly and critical, will watch.

I feel that you all, in some degree, possess these essentials, although on reflection, you may admit that concerning one or the other you have not yet fully attained.

Let me first of all name the concept of *stewardship*.

Every Salvation Army officer is a steward. The corps officer, the divisional commander, the chief secretary, the TC.

But the stewardship of a training principal touches on the future of the whole Salvation Army. It is a sobering thought that the young people you now have in your care will one day lead the Army in your territory, some of them in other lands, one or two possibly assuming international leadership.

In a very real sense you are responsible for what they learn, for what they accept and for what they begin to put into practice. Cadets are extremely impressionable. Very often they will carry indelible marks with them throughout life, not of what you said, but of your attitude – an aside reaction, a smile, a handshake.

We were 500 cadets in my session. Our training principal was Commissioner Charles Jeffries. But we did not see much of him except in big meetings and lectures. He had opened our work in China, and he loved China. He often spoke about that great country. But it impressed us more to learn that he had been the leader of the 'Skeleton Army' that fought William Booth and his Salvation Army on the streets of Whitechapel – until he was converted and became a Salvationist himself.

He was a 'he-man', a quick-witted Londoner, a man of few words, always to the point, who could preach about hellfire and the tail of the devil, so that we seemed to smell sulphur and brimstone! Towards the end of the session nearly all the men had had an interview with the Principal – but not I. I had almost given up hope of being called. Then one day, after a lecture at Mildmay, I was called. But not into an office. The commissioner was just ready to leave – putting on his coat.

'How are you, Wickberg?' he asked. 'What do you read?'

What a question I thought – and then I said: 'I read the Bible and *O&R*.'

'Of course, you do,' said the commissioner, 'what else?'

Again I thought: 'What a question!' But then I took courage and said: 'Well, there isn't much time here to read much else.' I shall never forget his reaction. He grabbed me with one hand, looked straight into my eyes and said: 'Wickberg, if you are going to do the work of a Salvation Army officer as you should, you will never have more time than you have here.' This he said and departed.

But I never forgot it. He probably did...

Our own stewardship includes our duty to teach the cadets theirs. And stewardship includes more than our attitude to money. It includes responsibility and accountability of time.

I think modern psychology has a great deal to teach us about our use of time. Salvation Army officers and leaders must learn to work and work hard. But it is equally important that they learn to relax. Archbishop Söderblom used to say that his priests should work themselves to death, but not in a year or two.

It is possible to get tense and remain tense, day and night, until something snaps. But before it snaps, that tension can make life unbearable for the officer, and his or her family, and all who work with him or her.

During my first year as a divisional commander I was so anxious to do all that was expected of me that I accepted every invitation throughout the division, Sunday and weekday, home league and junior demonstrations, and all the other functions. Until after a year I had lost my sleep. I couldn't sleep. Then I realised that I would have to space my work differently. It was not easy, but I learned how to become the master of my own diary. I have since advised many comrade officers to do the same.

Bishop Berggrav of Norway, the man who stood up to Quisling during the occupation, and was put in prison, used to be very much in demand for lectures and preaching assignments throughout Norway. Once he was asked to go to a certain town for a meeting, but declined. He was asked if he had another engagement on that date. 'Yes', he said, he had. 'Could we ask what that other engagement is?' asked someone. 'Yes,' replied the bishop, 'on that day I shall be playing with my grandchildren.'

Blessed is the man, who is able to relax! We must learn – and teach others – to relax anywhere, at any time – waiting for a bus, or sitting down between two lectures.

It has been said that the busiest people in this world always have time. They have learned to organise their time to cut out, or cut down, *non*-essentials.

Fénelon, the famous French archbishop, once pointed out to a nobleman how overburdened, and how racked and distracted the man's life was. How greatly that over-burdenedness damaged his prayer life. He advised the nobleman to begin his day with quietly running through in his mind the chief things he would probably have to do, or would probably be solicited to do, during the coming day. He should then reduce the number of such things as much as was wisely possible. Also, that when he came to the actual doing of these things, he should clip his action of all unnecessary detail and development.

> In this way he would succeed in placing each action within a circumambient air of leisure – of leisure for the spirit of prayer and peace. This would be like the ordering of a wise gardener, who carefully sees to it that the young trees he plants have sufficient spaces each from the other – have sufficient air in which to grow and expand.[126]

Principles of leadership

The concept of leadership is related to that of stewardship.

There was a time in the world of industry and commerce when it was said that *leaders are born*, not made. It was held that such leadership traits as honesty, loyalty, ambition, aggressiveness, initiative and drive were carried in the genes and people sufficiently endowed with these traits could lead others better than those less well endowed. Lately it is conceded that not by inheritance only, but also by learning and experience are leaders made. Now, we are thinking of *Christian leadership*.

There is a verse in 1 Timothy (3:1 *NEB*) which reads like this: 'To aspire to leadership is an honourable ambition.'

It has been suggested that not all Christians can accept such a statement without a measure of reservation. Should it not be the office that seeks the man, rather than the man the office? Is it not perilous to put an ambitious man into office? Is there not more than a modicum of truth in the claim that ambition is 'the last infirmity of noble minds?' [James M. Barrie].

Was not Shakespeare expressing a profound truth when he made Wolsey say:

> *Cromwell, I charge thee, fling away ambition,*
> *By that sin fell the angels: how can man then*
> *The image of His Maker, hope to profit by it?*[127]

But J. Oswald Sanders draws our attention to the fact that while leadership, even Christian leadership, today may bring honour and prestige, when Paul wrote, conditions were very different.

Then the office of a bishop or overseer, was not coveted by many. It involved great dangers and heavy responsibilities, hardship, contempt and rejection. In times of persecution the leader drew the fire, and he was the first to suffer.

Today Christian leadership – leadership in the Army – is often under scrutiny and often criticised. We are charged with authoritarianism and Victorian thinking. We are reminded that all men are equal. [Orwell's] addition that 'some … are more equal than others' is often forgotten.

The facts of life, of course, make it abundantly clear that leadership is still required, is indeed indispensable. We see it all around us, in politics and commerce and industry. But it is needed also for example in a band. The bandmaster, in fact, must be in absolute control of his band, or nothing worthwhile can be achieved. The police officer must be in full control, the fire brigade commander, and so on.

On the pages of the Bible the great leaders stand out, both in the Old Testament and the New Testament. Jesus is called the 'Author' of our faith, but another translation says 'the Captain' of our faith.

We all know the difference it can make in a corps, what kind of leader is in charge. We have all seen a corps almost grind to a halt under an officer who is a poor leader: most of us have also seen the same corps pick up, recover, increase under another officer, whose leadership made all the difference.

'Leadership' is a subject so vast and so important that it is worthy of a series of talks and much discussion. Here I can only touch upon a few aspects.

    a. Spiritual leadership differs basically from worldly leadership. Yet it does mean what it says: the ability to lead others.

    b. As spiritual leaders we must be able to inspire others, win their confidence and make our ideals and our goals clear and hopefully achievable.

c. As spiritual leaders we are often required to stand alone, to stand against a majority. Twelve spies came back, only two advocated immediate action. They were right – but their recommendation was not accepted (Numbers 13:30-14:30). Ibsen declared: 'The minority is always right.' But that is not always true.

d. The test of good leadership is the ability to delegate. He is not a good leader who tries to do everything himself. Even when we know that we could and would do something better than anyone else at hand, it is better to delegate, to train and to teach others.

e. A good leader encourages his people. Criticism may be necessary – but not in the first sentence! Some of our best officers, some of the most able, are not very good at handling people. They hurt people, often without even knowing it. They discourage people, they upset them. And then it is hard to obtain the cooperation that is so essential. Often it is the tone in which we say something that is wrong. Sometimes it is our face.

f. I sometimes say to the Chief: this man writes a good letter. Our letters reveal a great deal. A good leader writes a good letter.

Cardinal Heenan, the Catholic Archbishop here in Westminster, London, once commented on his 'boss' at seminary and said: 'His habit of treating students almost as equals did not ruin his authority. His informal equalitarian attitude, in moments of relaxation was possible only because of his self-evident holiness.'

How good, if that can be said of us. Unfortunately, some officers, some leaders, have lost their authority, their dignity, by always cracking jokes and always trying to be chummy.

To develop leaders means to spot leadership qualities in the individual and help that one to develop. Some of the early leaders were great originals. We have had them in every country. Today the complaint is that we have so few 'outstanding' leaders, original leaders.

While it is true that the Army may not be able to hold everybody, I fear we are losing too many, who might have given original leadership, if we had managed to keep the fire burning.[128]

A Principal is always learning

The *NEB* has an interesting rendering of Matthew 13:52: 'learner in the Kingdom'. 'When...a teacher...has become a learner...he is like a householder who can produce from his store both the new and the old.'

Some years ago the Rector of Basle University came up to retirement. One day a journalist came to interview him, and asked him what he was going to do when he retired. 'Oh,' said the rector, 'all my life I have been interested in chemistry, but I have never had the time to study it properly. The day after my retirement I shall become a student of this university, a student of chemistry.'

Well, some studies may have to wait until we retire. But we should always be studying, always learning. I know of one leading officer, who is within two years of retirement, but who is studying to be a doctor of theology, while at the same time doing all that is expected of him in a demanding appointment with a good deal of travelling. Quite a number of officers in many parts of the world have taken a degree without neglecting their appointments. But I am not thinking of degrees now. I am thinking of keeping an open mind, an enquiring mind, a mind that takes an interest in the things around us, in the things that interest the young.

When I was a young officer here in London, one of my comrades started to learn German. It did not come easily to him, but he plodded on. His pronunciation was shocking, I thought. But nothing could dampen his enthusiasm. He studied on the trains and late at night. Some 20 years later he was called by the General and appointed TC for Germany. His German was not perfect then, but how glad he was for all he had learned. He was able to converse with his German comrades and even to begin to speak in German on the platform.

Our internationalism

Training principals should be aware of what our internationalism means and what it stands for. There always will be those who do not know, and who can begin to advocate 'separation', nationalism, self-sufficiency. Some of our young people have never met comrades in other lands and do not understand what internationalism means.

In some parts of the world it is not always understood that The Salvation Army is politically neutral. Some enthusiasts would have us speak up concerning South Africa, Rhodesia [Zimbabwe] and Chile. While there can be no question at all where our sympathies lie – we are against every kind of racism – we at the centre must always remember and weigh carefully what any kind of official intervention might result in – for our own people, for the people we serve.

The same thing applies to politics within a country. We have members who vote differently in general elections and whose sympathies do not agree. And so, as an Army, as an international organisation, we have to remain neutral. This we must teach our learners and patiently explain to them.

Reading Guide

General Wickberg led The Salvation Army in a time of dizzying social change (1969-1974). When so many values, habits and traditions were being challenged, he attempted to steward change by embracing standards as he has described above while stimulating originality and advance. He did it all in the context of the intensity of the salvation war, memorably illustrated by his one conversation with his training principal, who told him, 'Wickberg, if you are going to do the work of a Salvation Army officer as you should, you will never have more time than you have here' [in the training system].

Here is a 21st century stab at applying General Wickberg's stewardship of standards and stimulation:

Salvationism[129]
- Salvation – fundamentally Mark chapter 1 verses 15 and 17 (repent and believe, follow Jesus).
- Holiness – unashamedly Wesleyan (that is, crisis is a

theological necessity, preceded and followed by process).

• Covenant – potentially transformative (the worldwide embrace of which will reverse global fragmentation and position ourselves such that God can accomplish his ends for us).

Cultural keys[130]

• We are a movement. While we are obviously part of the Church of the Lord Jesus Christ, on many fronts around the developed world the inclination to emphasise that aspect of our identity can be counter-missional.

• Salvationist culture ought to transcend national culture. We are distinct from the rest of the Church for missional purposes. And our covenant unity is much stronger than national patriotism.

Environmental keys

• 'Yes' rather than 'no'. We cultivate an environment, for that stimulates great exploits.[131]

• 'More' rather than 'less'. Our natural inclination is to do more rather than less in the great commission warfare.

• 'Risk' rather than 'safety'. The world and government restricts us with regulations and requirements. Yet we are a movement that risks everything for our great God and Saviour, Jesus Christ.

• 'Simple' rather than 'lavish'. Slum sisters and their incarnational service are the suggested model here. We must apply a different world view than the rest of society.

• Words have power. Much of the challenge from the enemy is verbal. We choose to speak life instead of death.

Cultivational keys[132]

• Spiritual intimacy – we want Salvationists to be on familiar terms with God.

• Mission initiative – we will not let the world or the devil blur our sense of, and commitment to, mission.

• Covenantal holiness – holiness and covenant are our two

essential characteristics. Married together they are spiritually explosive.

• Joyful humility – there are all kinds of streams within the Body of Christ. We Salvationists are historically and typically joyous in our expression. Let there be freedom in every corps and every Salvationist.

System keys

• The fellowship is in the fight. This is the most robust and intimate kind of fellowship.

• Deploy and debrief. Let's fight and then debrief. Let's learn in our fighting.

• Capture, train, deploy. Capture souls from Satan; disciple and train them up; get them fighting on the local front. This is our modus operandi.

• We love to fight and fight with love. Why? The love of Jesus in us never fails.

Means of grace

• Rations – we indulge regularly with God through prayer and the Bible. We lead by example.

• Discipling – we get trained up and we train others to win the world for Jesus.

• Evangelism – we cannot be distracted from this imperative. Again, lead by example.

World-winning keys

• Community.
• Discipling.
• Justice.

Discussion Starters

1. How can you steward standards and stimulate love and great exploits in your leadership?

2. How do these keys fit your local realities?

3. What potential futures can you unlock for your learners by using these keys in your discipling and training?

---

[126] Quoted from Baron Friedrich von Hügel, *Essays and Addresses on the Philosophy of Religion*, Second Series, 227, Dent, 1926.

[127] Quoted from J. Oswald Sanders, *Spiritual Leadership*, Moody Press, 1995.

[128] A long section about the command structures of The Salvation Army, the constitution of the High Council and other 'domestic' matters is omitted here.

[129] For more on this subject see Henry Gariepy and Stephen Court, *Hallmarks of The Salvation Army*, Salvo Publishing, The Salvation Army Australia Southern Territory, Blackburn, Victoria, 2009.

[130] For more on this subject see Harold Hill, 'Four Anchors from the Stern', *Journal of Aggressive Christianity*, 5-15, 64 (Dec 2009-Jan 2010), www.armybarmy.com/JAC/article2-64.html, and James Knaggs and Stephen Court, *One Army*, in *One For All*, Frontier Press, The Salvation Army USA Western Territory, Long Beach, CA, 2011.

[131] For more on this subject see General Linda Bond's 13 October 2011 video introduction to the International Vision at: http://sar.my/one

[132] For more on this subject see Janet Munn and Stephen Court, *Army On Its Knees*, Salvation Books, IHQ, 2012, and Olivia Munn and Stephen Court, *The Uprising: A Holy Revolution?*, Salvo Publishing, ibid, 2005.

Chapter 8
Training Evangelists[133]
by General Erik Wickberg
International Training Principals' Conference 1974

THIS conference is not just a routine International College for Officers (ICO) session. It is unique insofar as you all are in the same kind of appointment. It is important because as training principals you carry responsibility for Salvation Army leadership in years to come.

In convening this conference we have borne in mind two earlier occasions of a similar nature.

1. The first International Training Staff Council was held in 1925 and was under the personal supervision of General Bramwell Booth. There were 46 delegates from 30 territories. So important did General Bramwell consider the selection and appointment of a training principal that he made it a 'reserved appointment', subject to his personal approval. For some years he delegated this responsibility to Mrs Booth, who was known as 'the appointed officer'. The appointment of training principals is still the General's own prerogative.

For some years General and Mrs Booth cherished the idea that training principals, if successful, should remain on training work. They were appointed from one territory to another.

My father was chief side officer in Sweden, and Training Principal in Berlin and in Berne. It was thought that even differences in language and cultural background were less important than the choice of the right kind of leaders to train cadets. While fully believing in the importance of picking the right kind of leader for the position of training principal, my own experience has taught me that only in exceptional cases can a non-national adequately fill such a vital position.

2. Then there was another Training Staff Council in 1951, held here

at the ICO. There were 41 delegates from 28 territories, and the then General, Albert Orsborn, took a personal interest in that conference. He was, of course, himself an experienced training officer.

There is a quotation of his which is worth repeating: 'I regard the officer as the mind and soul of our work. He is also the main target for Satan's attack. The Founder was aware of changing values in the minds of his officers: "I see our principal danger is in our very best agents settling down...They constantly need stirring up and setting on fresh tracks. Lord help us!"'

And then he goes on, quoting General Bramwell: 'Is the Army going to be ruined like everything else, by its priests? No! Not if we can help it!'

As General Orsborn met his training officers in 1951, he stated the purpose of that council: 'We meet to restate, re-examine, clarify the particular aims of our training, which is as unlike the training of theological seminaries as our corps are – or ought to be – unlike churches.'

I could not agree more with my illustrious predecessor, and I shall be returning to that quotation a little later.

The most important development in our training operations since 1951 was the introduction of the two-year course in 1960. The document here is General Kitching's *Memorandum re: the Training of Salvation Army Officers* of 17 November 1959.

This set out:
- Organisation of the period of training, duration and pattern, but allowing for territorial variations.
- The curriculum, including new subjects.
- General approach to each period of the course.
- Balance of scholastic/practical.
- Pre- and post-training, and continuing education.

Evaluation of the two-year course

There have been territorial and national evaluations, notably the seminars for training staff of the four USA schools for officers. In September 1973 I called an International Commission on the Training of

Officers. The members were all experienced and knowledgeable and produced an interesting report.

I have to admit that I had hoped for something more radical in the way of recommendations, but perhaps this conference will come out with thought and suggestions that will complement that report. We have with us at least two of the members of that commission, and they may have something to say in defence of their report.

I need not remind you that no decisions will be taken here. Our training system is such an important part of The Salvation Army that any and all changes will have to be studied carefully by the Chief [of the Staff] and the General, and any structural changes, or changes of principle, would require study by all commissioners and the Advisory Council to the General, and a strong backing by them.

It would appear that most churches at the present time are considering radical changes in ministerial training – not just minor alterations to curriculum, but 'complete overhaul of principles'. This is understandable as we bear in mind the changed spiritual climate in which we live. Secularism and materialism have had a tremendous impact on religious life. Many of the established churches have seen their services attended by fewer and fewer people and their membership reduced. At the same time we must not overlook the fact that newer churches, such as the Pentecostals and others, have greatly increased their activities and their membership. The so-called 'charismatic revival' has not been limited to one or a few churches, and it may be too early to assess the lasting results.

Now let me refer again to General Orsborn's introduction to the 1951 Training Council: 'Our training, which is as unlike the training of theological seminaries as our corps are – or ought to be – unlike churches'. Let me repeat that not only do I fully endorse General Orsborn's opinion – [but also] I feel that unless we accept this basic view, we have not understood the fundamental position of The Salvation Army and, for very practical reasons, cannot hope to see any other policy through to success.

The basic position is very simple: we do not (and cannot) demand the educational standards for entry in[to] our training systems that are demanded by the churches. Consequently we cannot build up a curriculum on the same lines as they do.

The other difference is just as fundamental: our officers have a much more practical task to live up to than any minister. They must proclaim the gospel, yes, but much more simply, in a much more personal way and in much more varied surroundings.

They will be involved in 'community service', yes, but again in much more unconventional ways. They will be expected to meet people in all strata of life, they will be expected to keep up a certain amount of reading, to acquaint themselves with the conditions of living around them, but – and this is vital – they are called to be 'fishers of men', to seek souls and to lead men and women and children to conversion. If Salvation Army officers fail in this, they have failed indeed. If you as training principals fail to impress this on your learners and to train them to become evangelists, you have failed indeed.

Let me now try and assess the position in which we find ourselves as The Salvation Army today in 1974. While it is that we are still a growing Army, this is not the case in the many territories represented here. Training operations cannot and must not proceed in a vacuum. If in a territory we are losing ground, if fewer people come to our meetings, if fewer people are converted, if fewer soldiers are made and fewer candidates are accepted for training, and if the number of officers – active officers – is diminishing then, surely, we have to ask ourselves if our training system may have something to do with all this.

I would go further: I believe that in such circumstances we have to look critically and radically at our training work. Are the young people you are training now going to make any difference to our evangelistic impact in your territory when they are commissioned as officers? Will they carry in their hearts compassion and love for the sinners? Will they be motivated by something of the 'aggressive Christianity' for which the Army Mother pleaded? Will they feel some agony about the position as it is?

I am greatly disturbed when I think of our penitent form work in some territories. In Volume One of our history we read that:

> *One of the reasons given why some of William Booth's first helpers left him was that they did not like seekers being directed to kneel at a penitent form instead of being taken into an inquiry room... The method eventually adopted by The Salvation Army provides for exhortation to public declaration of the decision to serve God by kneeling at a penitent form – with subsequent counsel and registration, especially in larger meetings, in the quiet of an anteroom. In this threefold manner – by insisting upon a definite confession of Christ, by watching over and instructing converts, and by training them and setting them to work to save others – the problem was solved and the Mission's future as an aggressive organisation assured.*[134]

I am convinced that the Founder would furiously disagree with the attitude today by some of our officers – and some in leading positions. I came to one territory for some big meetings and when I gave an invitation to the penitent form in the first meeting, hardly an officer moved to pray with them and there were no registration cards and no pencils available. I did have something to say to those responsible! The excuse was that they 'had not expected a call to the penitent form in that first meeting'.

But I am glad there are also other territories where we are still true to our original calling. I would mention Japan as a model in this respect. I do not think that I have seen many other territories where both penitent form work and aftercare is done more efficiently than I have seen every time I have visited Japan.

In 1877, William Booth stated: 'In many of the old stations we appear, from the returns, to have had something like stagnation during the year. We have only got a net increase of 200 members...I should conclude I was out of my place if I spent 12 months at a place and did not leave it tangibly, unmistakably, visibly better than I found it.'

When some of his friends protested against the giving up of any ground once occupied, William Booth answered: 'If we find that we have made a mistake and taken a stand which is not likely to prove spiritually remunerative – in which the results do not promise to answer to the toil and sacrifice called for – let us have courage to confess our mistake, and withdraw for more congenial and productive fields of labour.'

Four years later he said: 'We tried various methods, and those that did not answer we unhesitatingly threw overboard and adopted something else.'

Wonderful! We are dragging our feet today, I am afraid!

The teaching of evangelists

Make no mistake, our social officers are also called to be evangelists and are often today winning more than the field officers – this is the ideal. We say: 'We are doing just this.' I ask: 'What are the results? Could we do better?'

There is one other aspect of our Army situation today – in some territories – that I feel must be related to our training system: the loss of young officers after one, two, five or seven years. I am not saying that our training system should be blamed for all these losses. That would be unfair and hardly correct. But I do ask that we consider at least two things:

1. If our training officers do not have the final word in the Candidates' Board to prevent unsuitable young people being accepted, then surely we must ask ourselves if we are sorting out unsuitable people early on in a session. When I was a cadet I seem to remember that we started with 170 men cadets; while only 120 were commissioned.

2. What is the image of the training system amongst our young Salvationists? In some territories it has been customary to arrange weekends for young Salvationists to experience our training programme. This has often been excellent publicity and has afforded an opportunity to answer questions and for placing the divine call before these young bandsmen and songsters and corps cadets.

And now let me deal with a trend. If we do not watch it closely and balance it well it will surely prevent our training system from fulfilling its original and its present purpose.

I find myself again thinking of General Orsborn's words of wisdom: 'The Salvation Army operates training garrisons or training schools and *not* colleges of education'.

I do not wish to quibble about words or terms, but I am anxious to stress with conviction and passion that unless we are successful in discerning and preventing the modern trend towards making an idol of education, we are doomed as a *militia christi*, as a Salvation Army. Not immediately, perhaps, but ultimately.

Please do not get me wrong. I am not against education. It is vital. We must have it. But we are called upon to train young Salvationists to become fishers of men, soul winners, not necessarily students.

We have become a little shy about our Army terminology these days. We prefer Sunday school to company meeting. In some countries the Army hall is called 'chapel'. Some *War Crys* are dropping the ranks of officers who write an article.

In such a climate I suppose it would be impossible to introduce the name 'battle school' in place of training college. But it is not a matter of words. And a change of term would not achieve what I have in mind.

We have always had within our ranks the so-called 'intellectuals', people with a higher education, and often they have been excellent Salvationists and models of humility. But there have also been some who have despised the 'others'. Often such comrades have been what we may call 'autodidacts', self-taught people. They have been intelligent, have worked hard at themselves and have acquired a certain amount of knowledge. It is difficult to generalise, but I am thinking now of officers who have built up a store of knowledge in some particular field (often theology), but have lacked in general education.

Often they themselves have not realised this, but have been proud of their new specialised knowledge and have succumbed to pride. They have looked down on comrade officers, who did little or no reading, who were not conversant with the latest trends in theology, and who therefore – in their view – must be regarded as unintelligent.

Here is a fallacy that we must guard against. 'Intellectual' and 'intelligent' are not always synonymous. I have known 'intellectuals' whom I do not consider to be very intelligent (*Concise Oxford English Dictionary* definition [1974]: 'quickness of understanding'). They are often specialists and often quite narrow both in general outlook and regarding other fields of knowledge.

Let me give you one illustration. I once had to say to an officer who could be described as an 'intellectual' that in his writings he was elaborating views which were totally unacceptable to very substantial groups of officers in other lands – equally good Salvationists. He then suggested that it was our duty to 'educate' these comrades! I took time to try and show him the background – historical, cultural and theological – of those comrades in other lands. Here was an intellectual with very limited knowledge and understanding of large and important sectors of our international Salvation Army.

As a Continental I may be overemphasising the advantage of knowing at least one other language – or at least realising that there are other languages! An 'intellectual' with knowledge of only one language is not very impressive if the virtue of humility is also lacking.

I would not wish you to think that I am now thinking especially of the English-speaking countries. We who come from small countries and whose mother tongue is not understood anywhere else must not forget that hundreds of millions of people in the world speak English. We must learn English!

Dr Clausen, who wrote a very good book about The Salvation Army in 1912, published in Germany as a doctorate thesis, said that there was no doubt in his mind but that the Army would become a world movement, for two reasons:

1. Its joy and childlike serenity.

2. The development of the English language as a world language.

'The future of The Salvation Army is ensured as long as these basic criteria remain intact,' he declared.

Unfortunately there are in these smaller countries (where often we have an Army out of all proportion to comparatively small population), officers who do not see the advantage of learning English. Often they are very good officers: fine characters, good on the platform, fine speakers and singers and successful in every way. But they realise that they may well be bypassed by others who either had a better education and learned English at school, or who were trained in London. They sometimes ask: 'Is the knowledge of English really the final criterion for a leading position in The Salvation Army?'

But let me also say that I know a large number of officers of exceptional intelligence who, through no fault of their own, have not had the opportunities of a formal education. Amongst these people we have a considerable number of well read people, balanced in judgement, strong in character and displaying that stamina, which is a vital part of true leadership.

I hope I have made myself clear concerning the danger of allowing our training system to become like colleges of education. But as education must have its place in our training of leaders, let me say something about the two trends in modern education which we, like all other educational establishments, are facing.

An American paper put it like this: 'Education today is in a troubled state. That is one point on which many educational conservatives and liberals might agree. One group complains that there is such a lack of discipline in the schools that students don't even learn 'the three R's' (reading, writing and arithmetic). The other group complains that the huge bureaucratic school system is too ponderous to accommodate the individual, especially the self-motivated boy or girl. Will the twain ever meet? "They'd better," says New York educator Marion Fantini, "or America is going to end up with such disorder in the classrooms that police will have to be stationed there."'[135]

This American school man states that about 70 per cent of parents are pretty much satisfied with the educational philosophy which stresses the basic subjects with knowledge conveyed more or less formally from teacher to students. It's the way they were taught, and it wasn't so bad. But they are getting vehement about permissiveness and lack of discipline. Other parents, roughly 30 per cent, are anxious to have their children exposed to educational innovations which they believe would make learning a joy rather than a chore. This includes the grouping of students by interested ability instead of age, dispensing with grades and report cards and presenting the teacher as a friendly adviser and companion.

We need not regard the figures given as representative outside the United States of America, but basically we find the two groups represented in most Western lands.

The learners who enter our training system have, of course, brought with them a very different attitude to teaching and learning to what was the case 50 (or even 30) years ago. Whether they know more of those basic subjects taught in all schools, is questionable. But they have a very different attitude to teachers and are used to discussion and questioning which we were not.

We must all be aware of the modern trend of 'anti-establishment', of opposition against every kind of authoritarianism. This makes training today much more difficult, but the clock cannot be put back and we have to make the best of the situation. Within limits, it may be true that these young people may make better leaders than we have been. They certainly are going to lead in a different way, with another vocabulary and possibly with a different assessment of human nature.

What we have to remember is that our young enthusiasts are still in training. They are not going to change The Salvation Army today or tomorrow. It is your task to show them how flexible the Army really is in regard to methods, yet quite inflexible concerning our mission and our ideals. It is your task to explain the workings of this Army of ours, not only within a national framework, but as an international movement with a membership of 2.5 million people.

It is your task to point out that our internationalism is something infinitely great and valuable and that the price we have to pay for retaining these links is well worth paying.

Training evangelists

An evangelist in the true Christian sense of the word is a man or woman who proclaims the word of God. This is reason enough why the teaching of the Bible has such a prominent place on every training programme curriculum. Unfortunately I remember my own Bible classes when I was a cadet as dull and unrelated to my task as an evangelist.

I knew all I had to learn beforehand. I had learned it at school in

Sweden! But it was not taught in that vital context of a prophetic message to the contemporary scene.

In 1967, Day Williams in his presidential address before the American Theological Society, described the current theological climate as one in which the locus of theology (and thus by extension of preaching and of the total work of the ministry) was no longer being considered as a study about God. For our modern world it must be the theo-sociological study of man. If we grant this premise, the meaning of man's life is to be sought through examination of what Williams called 'the justice which orders his social existence', rather than man's relationship to God in Jesus Christ. Such a basic attitude, of course, diminishes the need for study of the Scriptures as a recital of God's redemptive acts in history, and not primarily concerned with man, except in his relation to God. Then the Bible becomes simply another sourcebook for man's quest of knowledge of himself.[136]

The writer heads his article, 'Ignorant preachers', and pleads for Bible study based on Greek and Hebrew. This is beyond us – most of us – in The Salvation Army, but we cannot but agree with the writer when he asks: 'Is not the primary concern of congregations today the same as that of Zedekiah: "Is there any word from the Lord?"' (Jeremiah 37:17). The need for our time is nothing less than Jeremiah's answer: 'Yes!' But how can preachers give that assurance if they are 'ignorant' of the Word of God?

Now I would be happy to be assured by you that things have changed fundamentally since I was a cadet and that, in fact, the Bible teaching given in our training system is directly related to the preaching of the gospel.

I may have been a rather dull young man, but I have to confess that not until I was about 30 did I commence anything like a fruitful theological study (I read widely and studied many subjects, and, of course, I read my Bible and regularly conducted meetings for which I prepared carefully). And by that I mean a Bible study that sent me from commentary to commentary, from one language to another, from one translation to another, to try and really understand what the Bible message was – to me and to those I tried to reach. Ten years lost because nobody taught me and helped me.

Now there is in the English language such a wealth of good commentaries and dictionaries that our English-speaking learners should have no difficulty in getting the help they need – provided someone takes a personal interest in them and succeeds in making them not only interested but enthusiastic about the Bible and its message today.

In non-English-speaking countries the position is rather different, especially countries with a small population and with little or no Methodist background (our theology is, of course, originally very close to Methodism).

First of all, books, and especially theological books, are very much dearer because of the small editions. Secondly, Lutheran and Calvinistic books, not to speak of Pentecostal and others, can easily influence our young officers in a way that is anything but helpful. It should also be borne in mind that only a very limited number of English Salvation Army books are translated.

And so let me summarise: I would like you to think deeply and feel keenly about our present situation; about the Army and its mission in the world today, and about the role of our training system as related to what we are called to do: leading souls to conversion and holiness and service.

Are we aware of the danger of allowing intellectualism to dominate over the practical evangelism which must come first? Is the penitent form in the centre of our practice and our teaching? Is the teaching of the Bible practical and related to our ministry?

There are other big question marks in my mind as I think of training. Let me be quite frank and say that I have still to be convinced that the two-year sessions are doing all that we hoped for. Would we achieve more at less cost if we went back to the original nine months and then called in our young lieutenants for a refresher course of four weeks, or six weeks, after they had been out on the field for two years, or three years?

I used to say – now I only think so! – that then these young leaders would at least have in their mind the hooks or nails on which to hang the knowledge we try to impart.

In my old school in Stockholm there was a teacher who taught philosophy. He used to start his first lesson by saying that he regretted to have to try and teach them that subject, as he was convinced that as yet the brain cells that could grasp what he had to say had not yet developed in his young students.

Reading Guide

General Wickberg honestly engages with developments a generation ago in leader training. The means of his approach is an example for us as leaders. But the content is also worthy of consideration. He makes a series of statements that still provoke today.

- *'The Army operates training schools and not colleges of education.'* The content of training determines the kind of leader you create. If you send learners through a college of education you will produce scholars. If you run learners through a leader training school you will develop leaders. It is important that we remember who we are and what we are trying to develop.

- *'We have become a little shy about our Army terminology these days.'* The reticence about using Salvation Army terminology betrays a lack of confidence in our mission. Doubts about purpose compromise leader training. You will replicate who you are. If you are a confused leader or movement then you will create leaders who are confused about who they are.

- *'It was our duty to "educate" these comrades.'* The context of the quote was an 'intellectual' who felt obliged to educate comrades in developing countries who were taking exception to unacceptable views he was espousing. The condescending stance toward comrades true to Salvation Army belief and practice and a cavalier attitude toward it himself disqualified such a leader from legitimate influence.

Spiritual condescension is one of the sins of which each of us as leaders and trainers of leaders must remain aware. Dr Clausen's 'Two reasons for

Salvation Army success' are: 'Joy and childlike serenity' and 'English as an international language'. Well, English is the international language. But have we maintained joy and childlike serenity?

Discussion Starters

1. What do you call your training system? How do you see it?

2. What are you creating?

3. Is there any confusion in your leadership philosophy or identity? How can that be rectified?

4. How can you protect against spiritual condescension?

---

[133] This lecture was the keynote address and was originally entitled 'The Purposes of the Conference'.

[134] Robert Sandall, *The History of The Salvation Army Volume One 1865-1878*, 71, Thomas Nelson and Sons, London, 1947.

[135] *The Los Angeles Times*, 8 February 1974.

[136] *Christianity Today*, 2 January 1970.

Chapter 9
Men and Women Like Us: the Aims and Philosophy of Salvation Army Leader Training[137]
by Commissioner Arnold Brown
International Training Principals' Conference 1974

What were 'The Aims' in the minds of our Founders?
In a letter to William Booth (November 1877) [George Scott] Railton urged that above all else something should be done to train evangelists for their work. He wrote:

The importance of drilling the men we do get daily increases. We are not training one individual in our ideas and ways... The want of greater unity of thought, feeling and methods will continue to cause great losses with every change, no matter how good each man may be.[138]

[In a letter dated the sixth day of the same month to Bramwell Booth, Railton continued his theme as follows:]

I shall always, I trust, continue dead against any approval to a college sort of thing, which can never produce anything but parsons... we want to train men to be like us.[139]

In Railton's final letter preserved of this time he wrote [to William]:

My dear General... Yours is indeed delightful and yet embarrassing from the rush of likely candidates... The past gives us very little light as to the future because we are bursting out in such a way that another year will find us changed almost beyond recognition. We shall be compelled to do something for all this host of folks, with whom, if we

A Field for Exploits

can only drill and mobilize fast enough, we can overrun the country before Christmas.[140]

Toward the end of 1880, William Booth wrote in *The War Cry* concerning the character of the training:

In these Homes we propose to:
 1. Test the genuineness of the candidate;
 2. Teach the outlines of Bible history and doctrine, with something of reading, writing and spelling;
 3. Give some instruction in house-to-house visitation, street work, indoor meetings and all the measures peculiar to the Army;
 4. Give some instruction in home and personal habits;
 5. Seek to develop, encourage, and confirm the uttermost devotion to God, and of self-sacrifice for the salvation of men.

How were these aims realised by the Founders?

Firstly, the training period was at first very brief, sometimes only a few weeks. By the end of 1882 more than 400 men and women cadets had been sent out as officers.

Secondly, in March 1886 the training periods were rearranged. Instead of cadets entering at various times and being sent out to the field in like manner, entries and commissionings were made at six-monthly intervals. Each batch had three months at the National Training Barracks at Clapton (acquired in May 1882). This was followed by three months' 'field sessions' when cadets were sent out in brigades under the charge of training home officers, as many 'towns, villages, and hamlets as possible being visited and special campaigns conducted'.

The brigades were known as 'Flying Squadrons' (women), 'Cavalry Corps Forts' (men), with caravans to live in; a 'Speaking, Singing and Praying Brigade' (men and women) and a 'Flying Column' (80 men) who marched through Essex, Suffolk and Norfolk, knapsacks on back. Other marches took place subsequently. They were the forerunners of 'sponsored walks' – for God!

By the time the International Congress met in [May] 1886, 2,600 men and women had passed through the training homes.

Thirdly, there were variations in the system. In 1888 'training depots' were set up in various parts of the Central Division.

In *The War Cry* of 28 April 1888 the following comment appeared: 'During the six or seven months during which the cadet is trained, he passes a portion of the time in some depot, another portion in the field and a third at Clapton.' (Note: compare this with the current [1974] 'innovative' move towards 'on-the-job training of candidates for the Christian ministry' or 'Extension training for the ministry'.)

Later, the depots (renamed 'garrisons') appear to have been confined to London corps only. Shortly after, the depot system was abandoned, mainly to enable the training to be concentrated at Clapton, but also because of the undesirable effects upon corps which had cadets stationed there. All the work was done by the cadets and the soldiers were 'squeezed out'. In 1904 the term of training was extended from six to nine months.

Though Staff-Captain Olive Booth wrote as far back as 1924 of the need for a two-year training session, this did not happen until 1960, when the International Training College (ITC) and colleges in Canada, the USA and Australia introduced the new system. Thus we see why and how we began. We are required to build upon the foundations of our own history.

The aim encapsulated

1. The first aim – 'Men like us'. Is it possible to produce in 1974 and in the future, men like Booth and Railton? 'Only once in a hundred years, if then, can the Army produce a genius like William Booth' [said] General Albert Orsborn.

2. Men like us. 'Having differing gifts'.

• William Booth: He looked like a prophet, roared like a lion, acted like a General and lived to the age of 83.

• Railton: Self-effacing, committed to poverty; a St Francis who travelled third class because there wasn't a fourth; a St Paul who formulated the doctrines, and many of the *O&R* which he himself found difficult to keep.

But both totally dedicated. 'They have wholly followed the Lord' (Numbers 32:12 *KJV*).

3. The aim – to take dissimilar kinds of people, with differing gifts, and make them into people like Booth and Railton. 'Men like us…'
- Aflame with a passion for souls.
- Tireless and fearless evangelists with a world vision.

4. The serious responsibility of training officers – 'Men like us'. We reproduce in kind (the exception proving the rule). The leader of tomorrow will reflect the best of what he has seen and heard. He has no other ideal.

Illustration: when you look at officer losses, look at their training officers. What were their standards? How were those standards inculcated? The questions are endless – and important!

Training aims today

'The supreme object to be kept in view in the training work shall be the production of blood and fire officers; that is, officers possessing the Spirit, and able to sustain and advance the interests of The Salvation Army in all its departments and in all its spheres of operation' (Bramwell Booth quoting *O&R*).

Essential Aims

1. To produce 'blood and fire' officers. An inspirational aim, but non-definitive and non-directive. What does this mean in terms of function? The 'omni-competent jack of all trades'?

> *The great aim of all our training is to fit our officers for the work they have to do…training for the work of God should be adapted to qualify its recipients for that work…we say, teach the builder how to build houses, and the shoemaker how to make shoes, and a soul-winner how to win souls.*

(Catherine Booth, 'The Aim of the Training of Salvation Army Officers', written in 1884.)[141]

2. To ensure that men and women leave our training system as confirmed soul winners and sacrificial 'servants of all'.

3. To ensure that the leader-to-be knows his Bible, that he is convinced of the truth of the gospel, and that he has been taught both how to defend and to communicate it.

4. To ensure that he knows and accepts the Army's doctrinal beliefs.

5. To ensure that the leader-to-be understands the movement to which he is giving his life; that he knows and subscribes to the *O&R* and does not underrate them.

- A doctor-learner may be an accomplished surgeon but know little of the anatomy of the Army. The *O&R* will help.
- A prominent solicitor, speaking about the *O&R for Officers of The Salvation Army*, said: 'This book is a masterpiece! If only inspiration and regulation went hand in hand like this in the documents of many bodies whose problems I am called upon to resolve!'

6. To ensure that the learner has captured the Army's spirit, accepts its discipline, manifests loyalty, and gives evidence of total commitment. 'Join with me in suffering, like a good soldier of Christ Jesus' (2 Timothy 2:3).

Additional Aims

1. To provide such supplementary instruction as may help to fit the leader for the complex task to which he will be appointed.

'Training' versus 'teaching'. In the aspect of practical training, The Salvation Army has been ahead of the church college, but the system needs constant review. The training must be tested for its relevance.

2. To encourage learners in their thinking, in the art of discovery, in the necessity for making a creative contribution to the Army, in the harnessing of enthusiasm and the development of enterprise.

With a little wise encouragement your Training Garrison may become the frequent birthplace of new things.

(Bramwell Booth – International Training Staff Council, 1925. See also page 4 of this book.)

Illustration: The Cellar, Gutter and Garret Brigade.

More recently: The Joystrings; Salvation Army musicals.

3. To provide such educational assistance as may be possible (or

inescapably necessary) without losing the primary emphases of training. Training college rather than simply theological college.

In summary

The aims of training are to produce men and women who:
- Know God
  In holiness of heart and purity of life.
  In prayer, witness, service and sacrifice.
  In nobility of character and quality of life.
- Know themselves
  Their strengths and how to direct them.
  Their weaknesses and how to overcome them.
  Their intention, grounded in certainty.
  Their possibilities for good and how to develop them.
- Know their mission
  Understand the implications of God's call to leadership.
  Realise what the Army is and what it exists for.
  Share the burden of the world's sin and suffering.
  Desire above all else – above self, comfort, recognition –
the glory of God and the salvation of the world.

Reading Guide

There is a lot of controversy to chew on in the then Commissioner Brown's presentation. Here is a quick take on a few of the issues:

1. 'Men like us' – you have to have intestinal fortitude to make that statement. Not too many leaders are on the record indicating that their purpose in training leaders is to make leaders who are like them. But it is true. Paul did it: 'Therefore, I urge you to imitate me' (1 Corinthians 4:16). Brown does it here with William and Bramwell Booth and Railton. And the discipling process results in replication. People need a model of the Christian life. Our learners usually acquire traits from us, for better or worse. But it is an outflow of our theological confidence in God's good promises to sanctify us that positions Paul, Railton and Booth (and Brown)

to assert this goal. We believe that he can make us holy. And we want to make others like us to win the salvation war.

2. 'Overrun the country by Christmas' – the context for Brown's remarks from Railton was, statistically, the greatest revival up to that point in history (1878-1888). Railton figured that with the momentum they were experiencing, conversion of the whole country was within the realm of possibility! Hallelujah! This is evidence not only of the revival conditions that accompanied The Salvation Army into just about every country it invaded in the 19th century but also the apostolic faith exercised by the leaders. These heroes took God at his word and believed for even greater things.

3. Flexible training in the 19th century – 120 years ago The Salvation Army knew the importance of apprenticeship in leader training. After a period of centralised teaching, they deployed learners to local fronts with leading edge officers at leading edge corps. And the practical benefits of spiritual intensity in that environment refined character and skills for the lifetime of warfare ahead. It is a lesson with which we continue to dabble organisationally in various parts of the world. Where it is happening, we are the better for it.

Discussion Starters

1. Do you want to raise up leaders like you? What characteristics might you want to improve before joining the ranks of Paul, Booth and Railton in making that bold statement?

2. What can you do to inculcate in your learners a bold faith balanced by a great commission vision?

3. How do we develop 'blood and fire' leaders?

4. How can you intentionally implement apprenticeship into your leader training? How important is it that you are incarnational in that exercise?

5. What does it look like today to 'know God, know yourself, and know your mission'?

[137] The original title was simply 'The Aims and Philosophy of Salvation Army Training'.
[138] Robert Sandall, *The History of The Salvation Army Volume One 1865-1878*, 223, Thomas Nelson and Sons, London, 1947.
[139] Ibid, 224.
[140] Ibid, 225.
[141] Arch Wiggins, *The History of The Salvation Army Volume Four 1886-1904*, 384, Thomas Nelson & Sons, London, 1964.

Chapter 10
Contextualisation and Other Dynamics of the Smaller Training System[142]
by Major Paul Rader
International Training Principals' Conference 1974

MOST of our officer training programmes are small. Of the 47 schools throughout the world, only seven boast 45 students or more. Thirty-three have no more than 30 and just over half our schools have 20 or fewer officer-cadets in training. These smaller systems have a particular significance as most of them are scattered throughout those areas of the world where the potential for the growth of the Army may be greatest in the next few decades. Nearly 80 per cent of the smaller schools are in the developing world. Of the 29 schools located in Asia, Africa and Latin America, 26 have 30 cadets or less, and 18 have 20 or less.

In reflecting on the particular challenges facing smaller training systems then, the smaller school in the developing world necessarily becomes the focus of our concern. Hopefully, many of the issues raised will relate to the situation of smaller systems in Western territories as well.

Relevancy of training

Contextualisation

Smaller colleges, especially those in the developing world, are being challenged to re-evaluate the relevance of their programmes as a meaningful and authentic response to the gospel within the framework of their particular historical and cultural situations. An insistence upon such contextualisation has become the watchword of the Theological Education Fund (TEF) of the World Council of Churches in its urgent appeal for the renewal and reform of theological education in the developing world.

Beyond the necessity for an authentic embodiment of the gospel in terms of traditional culture (indigenization), contextualisation focuses on the meaning of the gospel in terms of the dynamics of change that shape the historical moment of peoples and nations.[143]

This concept speaks to the question of the relevancy of our training programmes. Do our curricula in developing world schools adequately address the issues in ministry or do they too rigidly conform to Western models that may prepare learners to answer questions no one is asking?

The Asian immersed in a context of shadowy pantheism, religious mythology and an understanding of the world as illusion may need to focus in their study of doctrine on the concepts of monotheism, the personal character of God and his redemptive acts in space-time history. In the West the accent may fall elsewhere. The Old Testament understanding of history, its concept of sin as a betrayal of divine love and a breach of covenant and its treatment of idolatry may be of far more importance to an African learner preparing for ministry among tribals than for Europeans.

Spiritism is a major threat in Latin America today. Some observers regard it as the most rapidly growing religious movement in this part of the world. If our training system fails to take the question seriously and leaders are ill-equipped to deal with spiritism biblically and authoritatively, not only will they fail to win those held in its grip, but also their own people may be deceived.

Whatever else the gospel offers, in animistic cultures, it must proclaim deliverance from the domination of spirit powers. Few are the African and Asian leaders who have not experienced direct confrontation with possession, witchcraft and sorcery. Many have been called upon to perform exorcisms. In some cases a direct encounter with the powers of darkness has been required to demonstrate dramatically the supremacy of Christ, releasing the people from the bondage of fear and resulting in a large-scale turning to the Lord. In such a context, Bible classes will need to probe the significance of passages like Colossians 1:15-17 that proclaim the power of Christ to rescue those in bondage from the 'dominion of darkness' (Colossians 1:13).[144]

Doctrine, *O&R* and field preparation seminars will need to treat the theoretical and practical aspects of the encounter with spirit powers.

The Korean *ch'udosik* [spelt phonetically] is an acceptable Christian functional substitute for the traditional rites of ancestor worship. As a memorial service of worship is conducted in the home, it satisfies the Korean desire to honour the deceased while providing an opportunity for emphasising the Christian understanding of death and resurrection. Without careful training, however, leaders may find themselves functioning as virtual shamans at family insistence, praying to the dead or pleading for their salvation. Guidelines are needed, but the issue may never be broached.

The whole question of Salvation Army ecclesiology is of great significance where the total Christian community is only an embattled minority, and fellowship with other believers is highly valued. The effort to distinguish the Army from the churches (growing largely out of the Western historical context) may be counterproductive if we fail to make clear how the Army genuinely embodies the reality of the New Testament concept of the Church and the churches.

Where whole families and villages are turning to Christ, in Africa and Indonesia, for example, learners must be instructed in the dynamics of culturally prescribed multi-individual decision-making mechanisms and how they relate to evangelical emphasis on individual conversion. Adequate field preparation might well include instruction in how to precipitate and consummate a 'people movement to Christ'.[145]

In much of the developing world, reference books and commentaries are largely unavailable to leaders. By training learners in inductive Bible study methods, they can be equipped to get into the Word themselves, analyse the content, interpret accurately and apply biblical truth to life situations. A facility in using these tools of Bible study may be far more essential than a comprehensive mastery of content according to a Western outline.[146]

One might like to ignore the struggle for liberation and justice in the developing world. But the issues are no less insistent among the troubled masses of these nations today than was the plight of 'the submerged tenth' in the England of 1890. Our position regarding involvement in political confrontations and revolutionary movements is no doubt defensible, but when, as in [South] Korea, six Christian workers have been sentenced recently to prison terms of 10 to 15 years for protesting constitutional reforms out of their Christian conscience, glib answers as to why the Army opts out of the struggle may sound hollow to the young. This is especially true when the salvation God offers today is widely being interpreted in terms of precisely this kind of historical engagement, and mission is being defined in terms of identification with God's saving activity within secular history.[147] These are only some representative kinds of issues to be considered in the contextualisation of the curriculum.

Structures also may need the corrective of a concern for contextuality. A smaller school may provide an opportunity for building a truly charismatic community where gifts are ministered to one another in love. Such a fellowship may become not only a pattern for creating a genuine sense of community in the corps, but it may also become a model of hope that demonstrates the relevance of the gospel of reconciliation for our fragmented world.

On the other hand, where a few people live in close proximity over a long period under a rigidly structured *regula* [rule] with limited opportunity for independent thought and action, as the Koreans say, the mind and heart can grow narrow. How can we guard against this outcome? What are the dangers of engendering a 'westernised' mentality in our institutions so that learners are actually educated away from the situations and peoples they are called to serve? Both the potential and the hazards of the 'life together' as the venue for training need to be explored in terms of developing world contexts.

Integration

There are at least four distinct though interrelated aspects to the training programme: 1) the spiritual, 2) academic, 3) practical and 4) what we might call the 'Salvationising' aspect, that is, the transmission of peculiarly Salvationist values, which are not only spiritual but decidedly institutional. The test of relevancy requires the integration of all these dimensions of training. The smaller schools have the potential for more easily accomplishing this integration than the larger schools. Where they fail to do so they provide a seriously faulty model for ministry.

Academic disciplines must be related to practical concerns of ministry, and the whole informed by spiritual values, which themselves are forged in the heat of battle and sharpened by disciplined reflection. The total process occurs within the framework of Salvationist commitments and standards which are tested and tempered in terms of the interaction of the other aspects of both training and ministry.

We are on target to centre on the 'heart'. But learners must be taught to channel effectively their enthusiasms, allowing their faith to be informed by Scripture while being matured in the encounter with the cold, hard realities of ministry and the requirements of Salvationist discipline.

Where such a pattern of integration is not set in the training programme, the ministry of the leader in the field will likely suffer from an artificial compartmentalisation. Such a ministry will lack both relevancy and integrity.

The need for working toward an integrated approach to training may be particularly acute in developing-world contexts. This is true first because traditional religious understandings are usually totally pervasive, affecting every area of life. If the impression is allowed that Christian devotion can be reduced to a scheduled activity, the Christian life becomes contrived, artificial and irrelevant. Secondly, in some parts of the developing world, the pattern of secular education is largely authoritarian with an emphasis on rote mastery of ill-digested materials. Little stress is placed on relating abstract principles to problem-solving situations.

The problem of integration needs to be approached from at least two directions. Instructors may make a conscious effort to relate the classroom material to field training, directly and indirectly transmitting spiritual and Salvationist values in the process. But it might also prove helpful for field training exercises to include opportunities for reflecting on training experiences in terms of the ideas being presented in class.

Field problem seminars can provide a useful forum. Perhaps the most natural vehicle for this integrative reflection, however, is the brigade. The group's leader can use its meetings not only for planning, rehearsal and evaluation, but also for consciously relating experiences shared to what is being studied in a formal way in the classroom. Written assignments and projects of this kind might well be required and then discussed at brigade level.

The potential of the field action brigade as a primary locus for spiritual formation along with the lecture hall on the one hand and the formally structured interview situation on the other, deserves attention. The small group can provide a unique opportunity for stimulating spiritual growth, deepening self-understanding, exploring new dimensions in prayer, learning to minister to one another within the Body on a personal level and applying spiritual principles to specific life situations. The smaller schools seem the logical place for this kind of experimentation, partly because limited staff often make it necessary for leaders to participate directly in every area of training with essentially the same group of learners.

Strategic anticipation

A relevant training system must anticipate priorities in ministry in terms of the overall strategic objectives of the territory. For this reason it is essential that such strategic priorities be clearly communicated through the Army system.

Training for corps planting

In most of the developing world, corps planting must be regarded as an urgent priority. Historically, a convincing correlation can be demonstrated between the numerical growth of the Christian community and the increase in the number of congregations. The number of corps, outposts and societies needs to be vastly increased throughout Asia, Africa and Latin America if our flesh and blood forces are to be strengthened adequately and our commission to bring the nations to faith and obedience fulfilled. It may be that an unrealistic model and mentality toward corps planting activity have been exported from the West. Where populations are responsive to our message every effort must be made to conserve the fruits of our evangelism by establishing growing corps, outposts and societies among them.

True, individual corps need to be strengthened. But the multiplication of corps is a matter of survival in much of the developing world. Patterns of corps planting vary in each situation. But in some rural areas, for example, experience has shown clusters of corps may be required for mutual encouragement, fellowship, financial assistance and united effort. Left in isolation they languish or require to be propped up by continuing subsidies. Existing corps must be convinced of their obligation to plan and nurture daughter corps. All of this requires training in the mechanics and dynamics of multiplying corps.

This is a specifically developing-world concern and one that may not be understood from the perspective of the 'post-Christian' West. Corps, in not a few areas, are being closed or consolidated and the emphasis appears to be rapidly shifting from flesh and blood to brick and glass, from praying, shouting, fighting bands of Salvationists to increasingly sophisticated (and expensive) complexes of community-supported social services.

It is the challenge of the 'Two billion without Christ'! It is the challenge of a world of villages, towns and teeming cities. A world where the currents of change are often rendering people receptive to our message, where corps wait to be planted, Salvationists trained, and the powers of darkness engaged in battle. Learners must be prepared to meet the challenge of this world.

Training for community development

Training for community development is a further priority. One thinks of villages where the Army has maintained its work for decades but has contributed little or nothing toward improving the lot of their citizens in any substantial way. The assistance that has been rendered too often has been of a temporary nature – emergency relief or dole-type charities. At best these efforts are timely and appreciated; at worst they are demeaning and resented. Most leaders are eager to provide more meaningful assistance, but they are often too poorly trained to mobilise limited community resources and work effectively and creatively for development. Specific training is required. Learners need to be made aware of government and voluntary agency programmes and how they can cooperate with them. In some communities they may become rallying points for productive cooperative effort, coordinators of competitive elements, and active agents of change.

In the revolutionary context of the developing world, a concern for development and competent involvement is essential in creating a climate of credibility within which the gospel can be heard and understood. While most will agree that Salvationists should be concerned with development, the question of adequately preparing learners for responsible involvement in terms of Salvation Army priorities in mission requires careful attention and constant review.

Training for world missions

One of the most significant developments in world evangelisation today is the phenomenon of developing-world missions. A recent study revealed that there are now some 211 missionary-sending agencies based in 46 developing world nations. They are deploying more than 3,000 missionaries who are serving in 86 countries and ministering to 65 different language and ethnic groups.[148] [South] Korea alone has a total of more than 245 missionaries working in 19 countries.[149] In September 1973 a significant meeting of Asian missionary leaders representing 14 countries was convened in Seoul. The conference announced the intention to establish a research centre for Asian missions and covenanted to send out 200 more Asian missionaries before the end of 1974.[150]

The Salvation Army's international structure and its philosophy of internationalism makes it the natural vehicle for participation in this new thrust of missionary advance. Probably more cross-cultural mission has occurred among Salvationists within India and Africa, for example, than we imagine. But the possibilities for the future are exciting. Korea has a surplus of candidates at the moment. Can Korea train more learners than it can deploy in anticipation of appointing them to missionary service in

Taiwan, the Philippines, Malaysia, Indonesia or Vietnam? Korean missionaries of other denominations are already at work in all these fields and more.

Such missionary involvement would give a whole new dimension to the Army's 'internationalism'. An internationalism that is a thinly guised paternalism and mainly a one-way street running West to East and North to South, is a product difficult to sell in these times. If taken seriously, such a new missionary thrust will require a broad base of commitment to mission at every level in the sending countries. Leaders must be imbued with a missionary vision grounded in a biblical understanding of the essentially missionary nature of the gospel.

This must begin in the training system. Bramwell Booth's urgent appeal to the Training Staff Council of 1925 is apropos of the contemporary challenge:

Can we make each learner see that this message, this living Word, is for all peoples?...what I am pleading for is that we should plant in the minds of these, our young messengers, the idea that what they have is for the whole world. It means catching a flame from the heart of God himself, who loved the whole world, and gave his Son to die for the whole world...How can you have a learner – or, for that matter, a leader – filled with the love of God and not overflowing with this universal compassion?[151]

Can we afford to ignore the implications of this appeal in view of the phenomenon of Third World missions?

Our cadets in Korea average 27 years of age. They will be 53 in the year 2000 (should the Lord tarry) with 12 years to serve in a century so different it boggles the mind. What will be the shape of Salvationism 26 years hence in the 'post-technological' age? How can learners be prepared for ministry into the 21st century? Clearly they cannot. Continuing education will become an increasingly important dimension of the total training programme. If the whirl of change has thrown the Western world into 'future shock' one can only guess at the shattering impact of change on much of the developing world. The pace of change is such that our carefully devised prescriptions for effectiveness may be obsolete almost before learners reach the field to test them.

Training for tomorrow must engender a capacity for openness and responsiveness to rapidly changing circumstances while securely grounding the learner in the unchanging certainties of faith.

Responsibility in training

Smaller training colleges, particularly in the developing world, face the challenge of rethinking their programmes in terms of responsibility.

Stewardship of the charismata

C. H. Hwang, a Taiwanese theological educator, has called for an openness both to the need of the world and the being and requirement of the churches below, and to the charismata from above, in structuring training programmes for the set-apart ministry.[152]

We are called to be 'faithful stewards of God's grace in its various forms' (1 Peter 4:10). Peter refers to those charismata with which the Spirit gifts those whom he calls. The exhortation applies not only to those who possess the gifts but those who are charged with equipping people for ministry. A recognition of the variety and diversity of these gifts requires that our emphasis be less on moulding learners to a prescribed image than upon motivating them to discover, improve and employ their particular gifts for ministry. The focus should not be so much on the instructor as on the learner. Training should be less a process of indoctrination than an adventure in discovery.

The discipleship training method of Jesus is the model. Jesus could teach on occasion with unique authority. When the disciples were stymied he made his meaning clear (Matthew 13:10-13). But apparently, he intended that the training of the disciples should proceed mainly on the informal level. 'He ordained…that they should be *with* him' (Mark 3:14 *KJV*). 'How long shall I be with you…?' he asked when rebuking them for their unbelief (Luke 9:41 *KJV*). And to Philip, 'Don't you know me, Philip, even after I have been among you such a long time?' (John 14:9).

His method was largely discovery-oriented. 'Who do you say I am?' (Matthew 16:15). The Emmaus disciples recalling their encounter with the risen Christ said, 'Were not our hearts burning within us while he talked with us on the road and opened the Scriptures to us?' (Luke 24:32, and 24:45). This pattern of training may be possible to a higher degree in the smaller schools. But are we exploiting our advantage?

Inevitably there is an element of indoctrination in training. Time is a factor. External patterns of conformity must be imposed to some extent. We are charged with the responsibility of preparing learners not for a freelance amorphous ministry but to work out their calling within a highly disciplined and tightly structured organisation. We have to come to terms with that. But we also must be open to the authority and agency of the Spirit in training. What is he doing in them? What is he giving them? How is he shaping them to the likeness of Christ? (Romans 8:27-29 *NEB*). A set approach must give way to a more flexible and open-ended programme intended to provide for the cultivation of the particular gifts and responsive to individual needs and potential. The ITC has set the pace in this regard. Many smaller schools have been unwilling or unable to experiment.

Sensitivity to culture

Responsibility in training calls for sensitivity to cultural differences. From the standpoint of our spiritual oneness in Christ there is a tendency to minimise cultural differences. But God himself takes culture seriously and relates to us in terms of the particular cultures in which we are immersed.

There are a few of our schools that are more or less monocultural. Some are multicultural. Most of our schools in the developing world, however, are in an important sense cross-cultural. That is, in many cases part of the staff (principals of about one half our developing world schools are expatriates) is foreign and both the structure and the programme derive largely from an alien cultural frame of reference. While this circumstance is to some degree unavoidable, a sensitive awareness of the cross-cultural character of the situation is required.

There are many areas where stress, misunderstanding and enervating frustrations may be occasioned by our failure to come to terms with the elements of 'silent language', the unspoken language of culture, in such situations.[153]

Teaching methodology is one such area. The relative effectiveness of various approaches to learning is not the issue. Patterns of learning are culturally loaded and when learners are suddenly required to learn how to learn differently, in addition to learning the material presented, their task is vastly complicated. For example, if they must learn to apply abstract principles to concrete situations when they are accustomed to rote learning and objective testing, we must be sensitive to this problem even though we insist that they accept the new pattern of learning. In some cultures where learning traditionally occurs mostly on the informal rather than the formal level, opportunities for such learning need to be expanded.

Whatever is taught must be filtered through the cultural grid of the learner. Dr David J. Hesselgrave points out that one must aim one's message to hit the mark in any cross-cultural communication: 'We aim well when we grasp the self-understanding of the respondent and address our message to him in terms of his way of viewing the world, his way of thinking, his way of expressing himself in language, his way of acting, the media he utilises, his way of interacting with his fellows, and his way of deciding future courses of action.'[154]

Viewed in this way, the problem is overwhelming. At the very least we must be sensitive to the difficulty, alert to the likelihood of misunderstanding, and responsible in our attempts to bridge the gap.

Scheduling is an area where cultural factors may impinge. Our understanding of the segmentation of time, the motion of time, points of time, progression in time, the appropriateness of certain times for specific activities – all of this is culturally informed.

Westerners pride themselves on their frenetic activism. To the people of other cultures they may appear shallow, impulsive and boorish. Rigid adherence to schedule may be a virtue in one culture, but in another it may be judged as being inconsiderate and insensitive to human and social values. This is an area in which the 'cultural distance' between village and city dwellers within rapidly urbanising nations must be taken into account. Where the requirements of training make it necessary to impose an unaccustomed attitude toward time, we must be sensitive to the tensions that might result.

Relational situations in training may be an occasion for stress. The Western penchant for open competition, for example, may be deeply disruptive in some cultures. This may be particularly true where husbands and wives are set in competition in the classroom. Direct confrontation is carefully avoided in many cultures. A face down on issues customarily handled through an intermediary may prove more emotionally devastating than the unwary Westerner realises. Various evasive manoeuvres on the part of a learner or leader thus confronted may be misunderstood as dishonest or deceitful.

It may seem at first that this is a problem only for the few expatriate leaders on training staffs. However, national leaders not infrequently are tempted to ride rough shod over their own cultural sensitivities in an effort faithfully to implement the Army's training standard. In some cases, what they understand to be essentially 'Army' or even Christian may, in fact, only be Western. The real task in all such cross-cultural situations, both for expatriate and national personnel, is to separate the universal essentials from the culturally determined incidentals.

Training for maturity

Paul's objective in ministry was to present every person 'mature in Christ' (Colossians 1:28 *ESV*). Ministry for maturity requires a high level of maturity in the leader. Spiritual maturity must be an essential goal of all training programmes. Such maturity is understood in terms of:

- Freedom: spiritual liberty, creativity, receptivity, sensitivity in love.
- Discipline: responsibility, initiative, responsiveness.
- Integrity: self-understanding, self-acceptance, self-confidence.
- Commitment: to God, to persons, to ideals, to structures.

The question is whether the training programme is calculated to encourage growth in maturity. It seems apparent that some patterns and relationships in training are likely to have an opposite effect, especially when they are carried over from situations where learners are generally young and single to those where they are older, married and experienced. Is it possible that learners may enter the college as responsible adults and two years later leave as emotional 'children'?

True, learners must be trained in submission to authority and prepared to assume the servant role. And when traditional teacher-student roles are assumed, the change in attitude may be dramatic, though seldom permanent. This role assignment may be reinforced by the use of demeaning forms of speech, customary when teachers address students.

In smaller schools the staff may be tempted to be overprotective, smothering initiative and self-reliance by conscientiously planning every detail of learner activity and providing for every need. After all, what is the staff for? The schedule itself may create the impression learners are incapable of using a free evening, or even a spare hour, constructively. House rules may also say all the wrong things in this regard.

It must be acknowledged that the maturity of learners can be threatening to the staff. As long as learners are compliant, mindless and dependent they are easy to handle. It takes a secure and self-confident leader to relate to learners as mature individuals. The least secure may be the most officious, paternalistic and overprotective in their treatment of learners. It is essential to strike a proper balance. Perhaps learners must learn to be learners before they can be leaders. But the goal of maturity must be kept to the fore. Learners must be prepared emotionally, spiritually and professionally for leadership that leads. They must be trained to train. The gifts of leadership are given so that the soldiery can be 'properly equipped for their service' (Ephesians 4:12 *JBP*). Is too much time given to training learners to do themselves that which they ought to be learning to train the soldiery to do? For example, in the field training programme?

Thorough instruction in leadership training techniques ought to be a first priority in many developing world situations. In India, for example, where in 1966 82 per cent of the population was living in its 550,000 villages, Army work is widely scattered. In north-east India there are only 371 active officers against a total of 2,075 corps, outposts and societies. Figuring roughly one-third of this number of officers to be wives or institutional and administrative officers, the ratio of field officers to points of field work is about 1:8! Obviously expertise in training soldier leadership is an urgent priority. Such training will do more to cultivate maturity than a constant round of 'hit-and-run' field training activities.

Systematization of evaluation and review

Responsibility in training requires a systematic approach to the evaluation and review of the effectiveness of our programmes. Such evaluation must be made in terms of a clearly defined purpose. In order to be useful for planning and evaluation, objectives in training must be reduced to measurable terms, not only in regard to examinations or learner evaluations, but in terms of the product we are responsible to produce. For example, what are the measurable dimensions of leader performance? Are such objectives regularly reviewed in evaluating the relevancy and effectiveness of training programmes?

Resources for training

Smaller colleges, particularly those in the developing world, face the challenge of resources for training.

Consideration of alternate models for training

In implementing training programmes that are both relevant and responsible, adequate resources must be discovered and developed. It may be that in some instances consideration should be given to alternate models for training in terms of the contextual requirements, the training needed and the resources available to undertake it. Modifications of earlier Army models may be more suitable to the developing world situation than the present two-year residential programme.[155]

A particularly attractive option is suggested by the programmes of Theological Education by Extension (TEE) being multiplied throughout the Third World. Beginning with a small experiment in Guatemala in

A Field for Exploits

1964, there are now [1974] some 80 programmes underway in Latin America alone, involving some 11,000 students.[156]

Training by extension would represent a somewhat radical departure from the present format but would be in keeping with earlier Army training schemes. In combination with a residential programme it might well be the approach best suited to the particular requirements of many Third World situations.

The basic concept of extension is to take the training programme to students in such a way as to allow them to undertake serious study without disrupting their productive relation to society. The programme is designed to meet students at their own level and equip them for ministry among their own people.

The main source of cognitive input in the learning process is provided by textbooks and programmed instructional materials which guide the student in assimilation of basic data. Extension is not to be confused with correspondence studies, however. The plan calls for regular weekly meetings with fellow students and an instructor at a nearby extension centre. The instructor helps the student hurdle roadblocks in understanding, provides guidance in reading and study, and stimulates the students to relate their learning to the life situations in which they are daily involved. The programme is most effective when students are engaged in some form of active ministry. Periodically, day-long seminars may be arranged at a regional centre or at the central school where library resources are available. These visits strengthen a sense of identification with the residential school programme.

Certain well established principles of education theory underlie the extension approach.

- Learning proceeds best from the known to the unknown.
- Learning depends on the prompt use of newly acquired information, concepts or skills.
- Learning increases when appropriate use of the new material is confirmed.
- Learning effectiveness is directly related to the perceived relevance of the material in the life of the learner.[157]

Even the most enthusiastic proponents of TEE readily admit it is not the only answer. TEE has fallen under criticism in some quarters.[158] But it nonetheless holds great promise as an alternate model for officer training…

Some possible advantages of a non-residential system are:

• It would provide for more efficient and relevant training in territories that embrace a variety of ethnic and language groups.

• It would help compensate for disparity in educational backgrounds, allowing learners to complete at least part of their studies on their own level and at their own pace.

• It would prove far more economical.

• It would ease the problem of childcare.

• It might well allow for more effective field training, more fruitfully related to course work.

• It would train learners in individual study skills, in a natural setting, thus providing a useful 'design for lifelong learning'.

Problems of geographic dispersion, cultural distance, disparate educational levels, language, finance, childcare, women's training and more, confront our schools in the developing world. Extension is providing workable solutions for training programmes of many other groups. It is recommended that serious consideration be given to the viability of an extension approach to leadership training in the developing world context.[159]

Utilisation of external instructional resources

Where the training staff is limited and qualified instructors are scarce among available leader personnel, the enrichment of the training curriculum is a matter of serious concern. In Korea a regularly scheduled lecture series opened to corps officers in the area has been well received. Competent and well-known lecturers are secured who make presentations on a wide variety of subjects related to the officer's vocation.

Cooperative arrangements with evangelical theological colleges that allow learners to take relevant courses in their second year may be a possibility. We are presently exploring the possibility of developing a sister relationship with the theological college of the Korea Holiness Church. We are proposing that qualified prospective candidates be encouraged to study there in anticipation of entering the training college. Under such an arrangement, officers would be invited to teach courses in Army history and polity as adjunct lecturers.

Periodically, seminars would be arranged at the training college for the Salvationist students. Scholarship incentives might also be arranged.

Special seminars provided by ecumenical and evangelical agencies may greatly enrich the curriculum. Korean learners returning recently from a Campus Crusade for Christ Leadership Training Institute were impressed by the intensity, aggressiveness, and discipline of their instructors, all characteristics they recognised as properly Salvationist.

The NCC provides a drama seminar each year that has proved helpful. World Vision Pastors' Schools and Billy Graham's Pastors' School of Evangelism conducted during crusades, may also provide a choice learning opportunity. In February, learners in Sri Lanka will attend a two-day evangelism seminar aboard the good ship *Logos* operated by Operation Mobilisation. Such opportunities can be of great value to the learners and are usually inexpensive for the school.

Concentration on staff development programmes

The staff members themselves are the proper focus for training-resource development schemes. In smaller schools where the staff is limited, leaders carry a wide variety of responsibilities. Spread too thinly they have little time to prepare adequately for the classroom. It is short-sighted to assume that staff must be constantly dashing about in a whirl of activity. Time is needed for study, course planning and preparation. A week alone away in a mountain prayer retreat during the summer break might pay rich dividends.

Training in teaching skills is an urgent priority. A teaching gift is a prerequisite for appointment to the college as an instructor. But teaching is both an art and a science.

Skills need to be sharpened and techniques updated constantly. This is also one reason why certain personnel should be kept at the college on a long-term basis, perhaps with sabbatical terms for study or brief interim appointments to the field in order to keep in touch.

Whenever possible, staff should be afforded the opportunity to attend seminars and lectures likely to improve their skills. The rising educational standards in some areas of the developing world also make it imperative that programmes for advanced study be arranged for certain key staff personnel.

The level of staff competence might also be improved if a concentrated effort were mounted to make available to the smaller schools materials, outlines and the like developed at the larger schools. Whenever a conference on training is conducted, results of the conference should be made available to all 47 schools throughout the world. It is hoped that the results of our deliberations here will be widely disseminated. In Korea we receive far more material from the TEF than from any Army source.

Two suggestions may be worth considering:

1. That regional follow-up conferences on training be arranged in strategic locations, to which key staff members would be invited. A team of well-qualified instructors might be assembled to conduct these conferences.

2. That three leaders involved in training be assigned as regional coordinators for leader training in Latin America, Africa and Asia. They might function under the direction of the Chief of the Staff, acting as clearing agents for useful information, perhaps editing a newsletter, advising on grants, programmes or funding schemes available through ecumenical and other agencies, maintaining organisational contacts, sharing helpful literature, channelling materials to the colleges and maintaining contact with one another. This could be done in connection with present responsibilities so that cost could be kept to a minimum. Some funding would be necessary, however. There is now no vehicle or agent for interaction between schools in our international structure.

Appropriation of spiritual resources

When we have done all that we can to contextualise our curricula, integrate our programmes, sharpen our skills and develop our resources, ultimately we are cast upon God and his grace in this crucial task of leader training. The larger schools have no corner on the resources of grace. They are alike available to us all. Training is an encounter with the Triune God or it is an empty sham. It is Abraham's Moriah, Jacob's Peniel, Moses' Horeb. It is the road to Emmaus, the upper room of Pentecost and the isle vision at Patmos. It is encountering Christ in the least of these brothers and sisters of mine (Matthew 25:40), in the little children (Matthew 18:5) and in our fellow 'sent ones' (John 13:20). It is all of this and more. In London or Sri Lanka, in Canada, Korea or Congo, only God can make it so.

May he grant you your heart's desire,
and fulfil all your plans!
May we shout for joy over your victory,
and in the name of our God set up our banners!
(Psalm 20:4-5 *RSV*).

Reading Guide

This is a classic by Paul Rader, a generation ahead of its time. It tackles issues that we are addressing today around the world. The summary is as follows:

- Contextualisation
- Integration
- Strategic anticipation

- Training for corps planting
- Training for community development
- Training for world missions

- Stewardship of the charismata
- Sensitivity to culture
- Training for maturity
- Systematization of evaluation and review

- Consideration of alternate models for training
- Utilisation of external instructional resources
- Concentration on staff development programmes
- Appropriation of spiritual resources

As we increasingly serve and fight in a global village, cross-cultural tensions and complexities are a part of our tactical and strategic warfare. Paul Rader provides a considered and field-proven philosophical base for our leader training, whether we are fighting in Korea, Australia or any other country in the world.

Discussion Starters

1. This provides a snapshot of the incarnational, missional, and spiritual dynamics at play in training leaders. What part do these play in your leader training system? What part might they play?

2. How do you deal with the charismata? Extremes include outright rejection – whether formal or merely practical – or uncritical embrace.

3. In Paul Rader's formulation, how can we be 'open to the authority and agency of the Spirit in training'?

4. What is the Holy Spirit doing in you and your learners?

5. How is he shaping you to the likeness of Christ? (Romans 8:27-29.)

---

[142] The original title was 'The Challenges Facing Smaller Training Colleges'. In this chapter footnotes in regular type are those provided by the author. Those in italics were added by the editor(s).

[143] 'Contextualisation has to do with how we assess the peculiarity of developing-world contexts… Contextualisation…takes into account the process of secularity, technology, and the struggle for human justice, which characterise the historical moment of nations in the developing world…It recognises the continually changing nature of every human situation and of the possibility for change, thus opening the way for the future.' Bromley, *Ministry in Context*, 20, The Theological Education Fund, 1972.

[144] Barbara Boal has suggested an outline for the presentation of this passage in terms of witchcraft, sorcery and magic to tribals in semi-literate societies. Her article, entitled 'Casting Out the Devils,' deals with the problems of presenting the gospel in meaningful terms in pre-literate societies and is based mainly on her experience in the Kond Hills of India. *International Review of Mission*, Vol LXI, No 244, 342-356, World Council of Churches (WCC), October 1972.

[145] 'People movements' have been an important phenomenon in the growth of the Army in the

developing world as, for example, in Nigeria among the Efik-Ibibio people 1927-30. John J. Coutts, 'Half Century in Nigeria', 20-21, *The Salvation Army Year Book 1970*, IHQ, London. A classic statement of the evangelical approach to the 'people movement' phenomenon is Donald McGavran's *The Bridges of God: a Study in the Strategy of Missions*, originally published by World Dominion Press, London, 1955, new edition by Wipf & Stock, Eugene, OR, USA, 2005.

[146] Detailed texts for the inductive study of Mark, Jeremiah and Romans have been prepared in programmed format by Dr Ross Kinsler of the Presbyterian Seminary in Guatemala. Originally published in Spanish, they are being used throughout Latin America and are now available in English from the William Carey Library (www.missionbooks.org), South Pasadena, CA, USA.

[147] 'Therefore we see the struggles for economic justice, political freedom and cultural renewal as elements in the total liberation world through the mission of God. This liberation is finally fulfilled when "death is swallowed up in victory" (1 Corinthians 15:54 *KJV*). This comprehensive notion of salvation demands of the whole people of God a matching comprehensive approach to their participation in salvation' (*International Review of Mission* Vol LXII, No 246, 199-201, WCC, April 1973. From the report of Section II of the Bangkok Conference of the WCC-Commission on World Mission and Evangelism on 'Salvation Today'.

[148] James Wong (with Peter Larson and Edward C. Pentecost), *Missions from the Third World: a World Survey of non-Western Missions in Asia, Africa and Latin America*, Church Growth Study Centre, 5 Fort Canning Road, Singapore, 1973. Also Peter Larson, 'Developing World Missionary Agencies: Research in Progress,' *Missiology*, 95-111, Vol 1, No 2, American Society of Missiology (ASM), April 1973.

[149] In 2007 the Korea World Missions Association, a broadly inclusive umbrella organisation supporting global mission initiatives from South Korea, reported 18,500 Korean missionaries deployed in 173 countries. These missionaries, with few exceptions, are working cross-culturally and are supported by Korean churches.

[150] In 2007, during the centenary celebrations of the Great Pyongyang Revival of 1907, more than 100,000 believers gathered in Seoul's World Cup stadium affirmed a goal of sending out 100,000 missionaries by the year 2030. The Korea Territory, for its part, at the 2008 Centenary Congress led by General Shaw Clifton and Commissioner Helen Clifton, announced a goal of sending out and supporting 100 missionaries by 2028.

[151] Taken from General Bramwell Booth, 'The Message and the Messenger', *Training Staff Council Lectures*, 10-11, IHQ, 1925.

[152] In 'A Rethinking of Theological Training for the Ministry in the Younger Churches Today', 11-12, reprinted from *South East Asia Journal of Theology*, 1 October 1962.

[153] 'Of equal importance [with formal training in language, history, government and customs] is an introduction to the non-verbal language which exists in every country of the world...Most are not conscious of the elaborate patterning of behaviour which prescribes our handling of time, our spatial relationships, our attitudes toward work, play, and learning...our silent language.' Edward T. Hall, *The Silent Language*, 10, Fawcett Premier Books, Greenwich, CT, USA, 1959 (also Bantam Doubleday Dell Publishing Group, New York, USA, 1988).

[154] David J. Hesselgrave, 'Dimensions of Cross-cultural Communication', *Practical Anthropology*, 3, Vol 19, No 1, ASM, January-February 1972.

[155] Major Raymond Dexter, EdD, reviewed the development of Salvation Army officer training programmes in his doctoral dissertation entitled *Officer Training in The Salvation Army: An Institutional Analysis*, 6ff, Stanford University, 1962.

[156] Wayne Weld, *A World Directory of TEE*, William Carey Library, Pasadena, CA, USA, 1973). Also a report on the status of TEE in Asia submitted to the Pan-Asia TEE Consultation, January 1974.

[157] F. Ross Kinsler, *An Alternative Model for Theological Education*, No 3, 7, TEE Seminary Extension 1973.

[158] A candid and objective evaluation is presented in the chapter 'TEE: a Critique of its Development and Method' in *Ministry in Context*, 34ff, ibid.

[159] In 1970 the TEF distributed copies of a 600-page compendium of materials entitled *Theological Education by Extension*, edited by Dr Ralph D. Winter, to all developing world schools listed in its directory. A number of training colleges should have received copies at that time. Though a great deal of progress has been made in the development of TEE during the past few years, this volume is still [in 1974] the most comprehensive introduction to TEE. A less substantial, but equally helpful introduction, may be gained from Ralph Covell and C.P. Wagner, *An Extension Seminary Primer*, 141, William Carey Library, Pasadena, CA, 1971.

Chapter 11
Our Future and The *Future*
by Commissioner Arnold Brown
International Training Principals' Conference 1974

OUT of all in this room, only Captains Akpan and Southwell and Major Booth will still be active officers when the 20th century becomes the 21st century. If Majors Rader and Tillsley are commissioners, and the retirement age remains at 68 years (which is doubtful), they also will just make it. All things being equal, as they say, quite a number of those present will undoubtedly welcome in the year 2000, but it will be as gerontocrats, as elder statesmen, as retired officers filled with wisdom – and perhaps a few aches and pains as well.

It is worth pondering, however, that some of the learners you are training will still be active officers in Anno Domini 2020. The second millennium since the birth of Jesus will not only have dawned, but will be firmly established.

Perhaps this reminder concerning the 'time stage' on which we play our part confirms what I have said in the conference brochure: 'No administrative activity of the Army more securely links the movement's present to its future, and, indeed, determines the quality, competence and passion of that future, than the training of its leaders.'

Comparisons and contrasts

In other words, the task is not only a 1974 responsibility, but it is a 2020 challenge as well. What will the leader we are training today be like in that future? Will there be the same differences as we sense between ourselves and our predecessors of 45 years ago? Or will those differences be lesser, or greater? Forty-five years ago, in the year of the first High Council, Army leaders included people like Higgins, Jeffries, Brengle,

Yamamuro, Hurren, Lamb. Their moral force, individuality, their spiritual power, their capabilities for leadership, are still remembered by those who came under their influence.

How do today's leaders compare? Certainly, they are different. They are the children of their time. They live and work in a world unknown, and perhaps undreamt of, by those whose names I have mentioned.

But if there are observable differences between the leaders of 45 years ago and those of today, how much more evident are the changes in the world itself. Science and technology have changed the standards and the style of living almost unrecognisably. In the lifespan of The Salvation Army transportation has moved from the horse and cart to the supersonic airliner. Communications have developed from the primitive wireless to instantaneous world visuals by satellite. Distance has been decimated. Isolation has been penetrated. The most distant point is only a few seconds away by telephone and a few hours away by plane. The mind has stretched and the earth has shrunk!

What of the future/what future?

What kind of a world are we training our leaders to serve in; in which to proclaim 'the unsearchable riches of Christ' (Ephesians 3:8 *KJV*)? If the past half-century is anything to go by, science and technology could change our environment, and the manner of life, in ways that we cannot even contemplate. Even if 'progress' is not so accelerated in the next 50 years as in the past 50 years, changes are inevitable. The unquenchable spirit of man for discovery and innovation has still to be reckoned with...and who can tell? The science fiction of our television screens today may pale away before the reality of the future.

My father was something of a visionary, a dreamer. I remember his telling me when I was a boy that the day would come when men and women would carry with them a kind of walking stick that would open out into a seat. The individual, once seated, would press a button and would immediately become airborne. He thought the concept marvellous. One would be able to fly anywhere at any time, he said. The stick would be powered by a force that would renew itself and, best of all, would cost absolutely nothing. As a wide-eyed youngster, I also thought the concept was marvellous, though I couldn't escape the vivid pictures that came into my mind of Christmas crowds coming out of the stores loaded with parcels, all deciding to become airborne at the same time. I imagined myself gaining altitude at about the third storey level and narrowly missing an oversized lady making a hurried descent back to get the parcel she had forgotten!

Fanciful or not, again, who can tell? It may be a far stranger and perhaps a far more wonderful world than we can envisage. My father often used to say: 'My boy, you'll live long enough to see people travelling from Canada to England and back during the weekend.' That prophecy, of course, has long since come true. We have even had weekend 'specials' from the other side of the Atlantic!

But it might also be a far more distraught and suffering world than we can bear to think about. If man's inventiveness cannot be stifled, neither, it seems (except by the grace of God) can his greed and his lust for power. These, alas, may bring scourge and sorrow. They could drive humanity to catastrophe and spell its doom.

So we really do not know. There is no one with perfect prescience. Our understanding of human weakness makes us fearful for the future. 'While people are saying, "Peace and safety", destruction will come on them suddenly, as labour pains on a pregnant woman, and they will not escape' (1 Thessalonians 5:3). We know that there will be no final righteousness and glory until Christ's reign. We also know that this is God's world.

'He's got the whole world in his hands,' we sing. And we who are Christ's are also in his eternal hand. So that whatever happens to the world, we who trust in the Living God will be safe, eternally safe.

But, meanwhile, it will be a changing world. Of that we are certain. Often I feel like amending the familiar lines [of 'Abide With Me'] and singing out of my tremulous uncertainty:

Change, and more change, in all around I see;
O thou who changest not, abide with me!

Out of the past some reasons for hope

The fact that the Army has not only survived, but expanded during its first century may well give rise to some confidence and hope for the future. The way in which new inventions and discoveries were made to serve the Army's purposes reflects not only the genius of its leaders through the years, but even more so the fact that, at the movement's heart there is [what Hamlet, in *Hamlet* Act 5 Scene 2 calls] 'a Divinity that shapes our ends'.

The introduction of the motor car, for example, led to the Founder's impressive motorcades. Thousands of people gathered along the routes, some to see the great Founder of The Salvation Army; others to see the Founder in a motor car; and, undoubtedly, some simply to see an automobile! But the impact was immense. Years later, General Evangeline Booth repeated this highway evangelism. One wonders if there are not thousands of villages and hamlets in various parts of the world that could again be stirred by such simple but well-organised means. A recent report indicated that the learners of one college found a bicycle cavalcade got them to new people, in new places, with new effect, and with new seekers.

Invention for spiritual ends

As with the automobile, so with the telephone, the magic lantern and the motion picture machine. It is worth remembering that The Salvation Army had its own picture production team long before any of the established churches thought about creating a media production or training centre. One thinks of William Booth's messages being flashed around the globe by telegraph and wireless in a day when to receive a telegram was a signal of incredible importance, to say nothing of novelty. Think how the minds and hearts of TCs were galvanised when opening a telegram to read in it a one-word message from their General: 'Others!'

Trains, ships, radio, television – all are discoveries which have served the Army, and have been made to serve its paramount purposes.

Surviving social upheaval

Another aspect worth remembering: social upheaval in the dread forms of conflict and war could have irrevocably shattered the Army's internationality, destroyed its manpower beyond restoration, and reduced its impact beyond recovery. But that has not happened. Throughout its century of life, the Army has been able to follow people wherever the exigencies and the holocaust of war have taken them. The Army's message has had acceptance in the trenches, in the foxholes, in the mud of no-man's-land, often because its ministry was a practical and loving one. When militarists dissolved the Army, it immediately rose again in answer to the trumpets of peace.

If the warlords caused band instruments to be buried and uniforms to be banned, inevitably they reappeared, phoenix-like, from the ashes and the rubble. The rage and the wounds of war could not stop the Army's message and its ministry. The sheer impossibility of maintaining a carefully-developed routine did not, as some feared, succeed in disrupting the Army to the point of death. Instead, there were new contacts; there were new services; there were new life-and-death reasons for dedication without a glance at the clock or the faintest thought for personal safety.

Arousing the collective conscience

Through the Army's first century the social conscience of governments and people was being awakened. The Army helped in this. When Bramwell Booth and W.T. Stead purchased a small girl, ostensibly for immoral purposes, they fanned public abhorrence into a flame that burned so hotly that parliamentarians finally had to raise the age of consent. In Japan the Army led the way in denouncing the white-slave traffic and in succouring its victims, until new legislation expiated the guilt that had been aroused. But it was not enough to fight social evils; social needs had also to be met. Not only were corruption and exploitation challenged, but compassion had also to be shown in homes, hospitals and hostels, clinics, dispensaries and schools.

Compassion, clothed in Salvation Army uniform, moved into the world's prisons and penitentiaries. What matter if the penal settlement were as far away as French Guiana, and as iniquitous as hell itself? As governments became more concerned about illegitimate infants, the lonely and forgotten aged, the handicapped and the incarcerated, one might have thought that the Army's business would diminish – that what Christly love had initiated, the welfare state would continue and refine.

But the reverse appears to be happening. The Army is more and more becoming an agency through which various levels of government prefer to work. In some parts of the world there are Macedonian calls from municipal and local authorities which only a shortage of personnel prevents the Army from answering. The fear held by some earlier Salvationists that in such service our evangelism would be strangled, that our interest in the spiritual well-being of the individual would disappear and that the Army would become merely a tool of the state has not been realised. What *has* happened is that the state has come to feel that the spirituality of the Army is a bonus that is missing in many other societies.

The Army serves the state on God's behalf

As the UK's Prime Minister Harold Wilson once said to me: The Salvation Army will be needed, no matter how elaborate the welfare state becomes, for three reasons. First, the state never discovers need. People aware of people do this, and eventually the state steps in to try and meet the need. Second, the state has neither the time, the money, nor the incentive to experiment with new forms of social service. Only people who want the highest good of the people can do that. And, third, no matter how proficient or comprehensive the welfare services become, there will always be those who will slip through the net.

'You see,' said the Prime Minister, 'the state operates by the head. But people are human; they need the ministry of the heart as well. If The Salvation Army can go on, as it has done, ministering with both head and heart, its future is assured – no matter how efficient the welfare state becomes, or whatever government is in power.'

And here's a thought that should not slip through the net of our mind: in the decades which have seen the greatest victories in the battle against poverty, starvation and disease; in the period when prisons have been humanised beyond the highest hopes of Elizabeth Fry and John Howard; when a man can have almost as much money in his pocket whether he is employed or unemployed; in a period when, according to the pessimists, our practical Salvationism would disappear, the work of the Army has expanded to an extent that William Booth never glimpsed in his lifetime, nor ever thought would be possible 62 years after his promotion to Glory! What is evident is that while old forms of need, and old forms of service evaporate, new forms of need and new forms of service are continually emerging.

The Army pioneered in caring for the unmarried mother. In those days, to have an illegitimate child meant the rejection of outraged parents and relatives, and the cruelty of a vindictive society. Today, the Army must care in other ways for mother and baby, no longer ostracised or stigmatised, but still requiring new kinds of understanding and assistance.

So the Army has survived and grown, affected by technological development but using technology wherever and whenever it could advantageously do so. A growing professional interest in the needs of man himself, his health, his home, his work, his leisure, has meant the taking of new roads of service. Wars and rumours of war which threatened to fragment the movement into unmendable bits and pieces have meant a closer binding of those serving and those served.

The winds of theology blow – past us!

The past century also reminds us that the Army has survived many winds of theological change. Theology is so changeable that it can often be confused with meteorology! There have been the freezing blasts of higher criticism; the chilling rains of liberalism; the swirling tempests of hyperfundamentalism; the grey clouds of social-gospelism; the dampness of 'God is Dead'-ism. To the list could be added a score of variants that have darkened the scene; neo-orthodoxy, radical conservatism, worldly Christianity and so on. But has the Army's simple faith, to which

Salvationists tenaciously cling, ever been more appealing to the world than it is today?

Under God, the Army was bequeathed a philosophy and a function that is the envy of many of the historic church bodies. The duality of structure which is the distinction and glory of the Army has proven its implicit strength and durability. On the one hand, the Army is a church, a denomination, a sect, if you like; on the other, it is the world's single largest welfare movement. The spiritual impulses of the one issue in the compassion of the other. But the two are indissolubly interrelated, interpenetrated. One without the other means far less than being half effective. One without the other means the end of The Salvation Army!

On this point I never tire of repeating the words of General Frederick Coutts, spoken in the Royal Albert Hall in the gracious presence of Her Majesty Queen Elizabeth II, during the inaugural meeting of the Centenary celebrations [in 1965]. 'If we ourselves, for want of a better way of speaking, refer to our evangelical work and also to our social work, it is not that these are two distinct entities which could operate the one without the other. They are but two activities of the one and the same salvation which is concerned with the total redemption of man. Both rely upon the same divine grace. Both are inspired by the same motive. Both have the same end in mind. And as the gospel has joined them together we do not propose to put them asunder'.[160]

There, then, is a dual structure with a single purpose – the glorification of God through both proclamation and service. As long as that shining idea is understood and nurtured, so long will The Salvation Army be undisturbed by the changing fashions of speculative religious thought. Our anchor will be the simplicity of our faith, unswervingly held, simply expressed, and undeniably reflected in our daily living.

The storm of schism

We have our anchor, but sometimes the boat itself has been mercilessly rocked. Not only have we survived and grown despite a technology which has worked its problems as well as its triumphs into the fabric of society;

not only have we continued to develop despite changed mores and, what is more, to increase our services to those who still find themselves in difficulty; not only have we held our own, and been requested to hold more than our own, in a changing social services scene in many parts of the world; but we have sailed on despite the tempests that have sometimes shaken our ship from masthead to keel.

There are splinter Salvation Armies in Sweden and in the Netherlands even today. The Free Salvation Army which for many years functioned in the Camberwell area of London, has only recently had its last meeting, with death attributable to malnutrition – no penitents, no recruits.

In Canada, in 1892, the Army passed through a hurricane of misunderstanding, with the loss of hundreds of fine officers and soldiers. In those days there were also the problems of the Founder's own family which could not be contained within the domestic circle. They were problems of leadership in which strong minds contended for specific points of view. They were not problems of immorality or dishonesty, or of other sensational 'skeleton in the cupboard' variety, simply disagreements on what was to be done, and how it was to be done. Yet the heat of those clashes warmed tempers for and against.

One does not have to look back farther than three or four years to recall the storm generated by a British officer who broke his word and then took the Army to the public whipping post through press, radio and television. The Army ship tossed violently, and some on board were genuinely sick, but the vessel ploughed on and finally reached calmer waters. Best of all, the cargo of principle and integrity was undamaged. It was a distressing case of 'man overboard' but those still on board pray that the one who created that particular storm will not be lost in it, but will find his own safe harbour at the end.

So much for a reassuring past. Evidently our movement can survive the physical changes that surround it. What we cannot stand is to be sapped of our spirituality. What will endanger us is to allow our faith and works to get out of balance. When that happens the whole structure loses its equilibrium, or, to return to our earlier simile, the ship will begin to sink.

The future – fascinating or fearful?

But what of that unknown, uncertain future? What kind of a world will it really be? We sense intuitively that it will be one of increased mobility. There are illustrations of this within the Army itself. Forty-five years ago officers serving overseas went for long periods. There were protracted and tearful farewells. After all, the appointment was halfway round the world, and during the lengthy absence there could quite conceivably be the death of one or more members of the family. To 'sacrifice family and home' was more than a poetic expression. Now, leaders serving overseas can have the advantage of excursion air fares that allow them to return home every year for their annual furlough.

To what quality of dedication will such advantages lead us? I give you another illustration. Candidates in these days look around the Army world and choose the college in which they wish to be trained. Transportation is no problem. Mobility is part of the lifestyle. I do not know the answer, but I suspect that only wise legislation will prevent us having a crowded college in New York in 1980, with empty colleges in New Zealand and Hong Kong, if New York is the 'in' centre that year, or a crowded college in London in 1995, with empty colleges in North America, if London happens to be the 'in' centre for training in 1995.

Mobility may increase to such a degree that the University of Humanity which William Booth dreamt of may eventually be instituted. To it will come learners from all parts of the world. Size would not be an insurmountable problem. The total enrolment would not likely be more than that of many a smaller university. One can imagine a collegiate type of university with learners of many nations taking advantage of specialist courses offered by various colleges on the campus.

Travel could then be so easy that frequent returns to the home territory for campaigns and, certainly for commissioning and appointment, would be a simple and speedy matter. And if my father's chairplane is invented, there would be no cost!

With increased mobility will obviously come increased leisure, higher standards of learning and many other aspects that will enrich the life if properly assimilated, or lead to unimagined ruin if improperly appropriated.

The future and God

Will our leaders of the 21st century be meeting people who will want to know more, or less, about God? My experience and observation lead me to the conclusion that it is much easier to talk to people about Jesus in these days than it was 40 years ago. Will that trend continue?

We should pray that it will! Those who 'discern the times' say that already reaction is setting in against permissiveness. If history is truly cyclic, as many believe, does this mean that the pendulum will swing from present permissiveness to future puritanism, or neo-puritanism? Does it mean that our leaders at the turn of the century will be facing crowds of people who have moved from indifference to religion to interest in religion? Does it mean that humanity will reject the worship of man and welcome a prophetic voice that shows them again how to worship God?

We are used to bracketing together the words 'time' and 'space'. So far we have only speculated on the subject of time. But will a dramatically new space age have dawned by the time the millennium turns? Will man actually be making 'his nest among the stars' (as Obadiah 1:4 puts it), moving with speed and comfort through the silent galaxies? In a new humility will he be led to exclaim with the Psalmist, 'The heavens declare the glory of God; the skies proclaim the work of his hands' (Psalm 19:1). Will it be a day when we no longer think of hemispheres and continents, but of galactic spaces populated with universe upon universe? In such a day, when computers will matter so much, will cathedrals matter at all?

Our speculation ends/we 'see the unseen'

Now let me bring together the strands of this strange, speculative reflection. Our primary concern is that we are now training leaders who must love and serve Jesus Christ and humanity in a world that is constantly changing and which in the 21st century may be changed beyond all our imagining. It may be in an improved world with unimproved people. It may be in a world in agony, yet populated with more spiritually sensitive people.

We cannot tell. If there still is a world, it will have moved that much nearer the time of Christ's appointed reign. Assuming that 'the end is not yet' (Matthew 24:6 *KJV*), what we do realise is that our leaders of the 21st century will need to be more spiritual than we have been, more flexible, more adaptable, more discerning. Dare we say that their love for Christ must match ours – or surpass it?

Whatever the future, we must teach our learners of today and tomorrow – the leaders of that future towards which we are inexorably racing – to know the difference between the things that are 'seen' and the things that are ' not seen'; 'for the things which are seen are temporal; but the things which are not seen are eternal' (2 Corinthians 4:18 *KJV*). Our work, and their work, has to do not only with time, but with eternity. May the God of that eternity be our strength and illumination!

Reading Guide

General Brown was a true visionary. His lecture from a full generation ago still startles with its far-sightedness. His main point is that we have to train leaders now who will be adaptable enough to lead in what will inevitably be significantly different environments in years to come. How do you train for change?

We probably need to leave space for the unexpected. If everything is so regimented that the Holy Spirit has no opportunity to interrupt, we might end up stifling our learners such that they lack the broad perspective, ingenuity, and creativity to respond to new challenges. But we probably also need to celebrate the unexpected. When I [Stephen] was in Victoria, Australia, bush fires threw Salvationist schedules out of the window and they responded with sacrificial resourcefulness to the crisis of multiple fires and massive destruction. From a leader-training standpoint it was not a distraction but a divine training appointment, providing what could not be scheduled or planned – an emergency that threatened the status quo. Learners who served through this experience now have galvanised in their spirits an abandonment to the cause that supplants routine and status quo.

General Brown also tackles the issue of relationship with the government. Here is the takeaway:

'As Prime Minister Harold Wilson once said to me: The Salvation Army will be needed, no matter how elaborate the welfare state becomes, for three reasons. First, the state never discovers need. People aware of people do this, and eventually the state steps in to try and meet the need. Second, the state has neither the time, the money, nor the incentive to experiment with new forms of social service. Only people who want the highest good of the people can do that. And, third, no matter how proficient or comprehensive the welfare services become, there will always be those who will slip through the net.

'You see,' said the Prime Minister, 'the state operates by the head. But people are human; they need the ministry of the heart as well. If The Salvation Army can go on, as it has done, ministering with both head and heart, its future is assured – no matter how efficient the welfare state becomes, or whatever government is in power.'

This is an issue fraught with tension. We certainly need both head and heart – discernment and zeal – to engage those in need with integrity.

Discussion Starters

1. How adaptable are your learners?
2. How adaptable is your leader training?
3. How can we prepare for the unexpected?
4. How can we, as leaders, best deal with the government?

---

[160] Various, *Into The Second Century*, 15-16, Salvationist Publishing & Supplies (SP&S), London, 1965.

Chapter 12
A Theology of Officership
by Colonel Eva Burrows
International Training Principals' Conference 1974

Introduction

THERE has been in recent years an intense and growing interest in the question of what officership is, what authority an officer has, what his or her role is in an increasingly complex society where the multiplicity of functions he or she must perform causes conflict and uncertainty. Questions being asked:

- If we accept the New Testament concept of the priesthood of all believers, what is the difference between an officer and a soldier?
- What is the significance of our calling and commissioning?
- Is the meaning of ministry the same for all officers – whether in corps, in administration, in social service?

The following, and similar topics, have been the subject of articles in *The Officer* magazine over the past few years from officers of several territories:

- Have we a doctrine of the Church?
- The authority of our ministry.
- Short-term commissions (which sparked off a lively correspondence).
- Functional ministry.

In January 1974, the editorial asked the question: Do we accept that there is a theology of Christian ministry, and therefore of Salvation Army officership, and if we do, how should we define it?

If it is officers only who are asking these questions, perhaps it indicates a fear that our 'officership status' is being threatened. Alternatively it may indicate a healthy desire to rid our movement of any tendency to develop a superior officer caste, a 'professional' ministry.

The International Commission on the Training of Officers touched on this matter. Members, while realising that time and the terms of reference did not allow discussion during the commission itself, expressed the hope that the theology of officership would be looked into, especially as it impinged on our aims and style of training.

Who needs a theology of officership?

It is necessary for our soldiery to have a deeper understanding of what officership is. In many cases they need to be educated anew to see the purposes of the officer's ministry and their own ministry and the relationship between them. Many need to realise that the officer's calling as 'servant of all' does not mean he or she is to be the general handyman/woman for all.

General Wilfred Kitching, addressing soldiers in an article entitled 'The Salvationist and his Officer', wrote:

The Army needs officers who understand the prophetic ministry, but every soldier must give his officer full and ready response. Soldiers who fail to realise their obligations as co-workers with those who have been appointed can be out of step in the march. In the set-up of our corps the relationship of soldiers to their officers is something apart and different from the usually understood relationship of a congregation with its minister.

Examples of attitudes of soldiers:

- A bandsman overheard discussing the three-day working week introduced during the emergency situation in Britain [in the early 1970s]: 'I don't know about a three-day week. I think I'll be an officer. He only has a one-day working week.'

- The corps sergeant-major of a large corps, unofficered for nine months, explained the awakened understanding of the meaning of officership among the soldiery and a new awareness of sharing in the total ministry of the corps.

Officers have expressed the need to clarify their role and the divine basis of their ministry. They suffer from 'role confusion'. Whereas Scripture requires 'some to be evangelists, some shepherds, some teachers and leaders', the Army requires the officer to be all at once. Then he or she may be called on as a social worker in the community, a pastoral counsellor. What are his or her priorities, as someone called to preach the word?

The Salvation Army has made the call to the ministry of great significance, but have we given attention to the understanding of the working out of the calling and the scriptural basis of the purposes of our service?

Examples:

- In the USA, after an intensive study by a commission, an official statement redefining [and entitled] *The Role of the Corps Officer in the United States of America* provides the corps officer with a clearer conception of his or her role in the light of changed and changing conditions. It outlines his or her 'master role' (as evangelist) and 'practitioner roles' in the community, pointing out that in effective officership there must be integration of both. This fine statement deals mainly with the functions of officership.

- In field officers' councils in Britain this matter was raised in discussion, with the resultant request that 'an examination be made of the biblical doctrine of ministry and its bearing on the training, deployment and role of the officer today'. This goes further than a clarification of function and into a scriptural study of the total meaning of officership.

In the ecumenical situation there is a need for officers to be informed about and convinced of the distinctive place of The Salvation Army in the church and a recognition of their officership as of equal validity with that of any other minister.

Because officers are not 'ordained', are they thought of as laymen by the clergy? In parts of Africa, officers are classed as 'evangelists' and not as 'ministers' for the same reason. But no officer is an inferior, second class minister despite the fact that he or she has not received the laying on of hands. And he or she must be able to articulate his or her convictions from the basis of Scripture.

General Frederick Coutts, on taking up office, gave as one of the points of his 'General's Affirmation', the need to confirm the faith of the Army in its place and function in the Church universal. He stressed the need to acknowledge every officer – man or woman, married or single, as:

> '...a good minister of Christ Jesus, nourished in the words of the faith, and of good doctrine' (1 Timothy 4:6 ASV). To insist on such recognition is not to want to turn our officers into ministers (in the denominational sense of the word), but to save any from grasping at a clerical collar as if it were a lifebelt which alone could win a more perfect acceptance of their service in the sight of God. No blessing – episcopal or non-episcopal – can make us more truly what by divine ordination we now are: ministers of grace.

(*The Officer*, January 1964)

This 'divine ordination', this 'ordination of the bleeding hands' as General Albert Orsborn expressed it, gives every officer equal claim to an ordained ministry with the ministers of any of the historic churches.

What is meant by a theology of officership?

The purists among us may quarrel with the term 'theology' in this connotation. However it is used here in the sense of applied theology – practical theology. This is not the direct study of God himself and his plan of salvation but is concerned with the expression of faith in our everyday experience, with the outworking of faith in the community of believers and with the application of faith in the institutional Church – the field of ethics.

So we have a theology of the Church, a theology of the ministry and moral theology. In these days there is an even wider use in such expressions as: a theology of the laity, a theology of change, a theology of prayer and even a theology of women's ministry.

In such a manner is the term 'theology of officership' being used. I realise that Salvationists with their historical emphasis on a practical religion have always been suspicious of the word 'theology', and no doubt many find the term 'theology of officership' very un-Army, therefore questionable. Perhaps we'd better say 'doctrine of officership'.

Whatever the terminology, the need is being expressed for us to look at the purpose of our existence and function as an 'Army' within the Church, not on historical or social or cultural grounds, but on theological grounds based in Scripture and on the guidance of the Holy Spirit in experience, which has given authority to our movement and to our ministers – our officers.

Many of you hold clear, personal convictions on this, and in the words of our leaders similar convictions are expressed also, but it is not possible to put one's hands on an explicit, authoritative statement. This would involve considerable research; perhaps initiated by such a group as the Doctrine Council. However, let us see what we can find.

Where can we discover our doctrine of officership?
In our doctrine book?

Here we find no mention of officership; not even a discussion of the nature, function and purpose of the ministry. Someone will hasten to remind me that the new [1969] *Handbook of Doctrine* includes a short section which might be termed our theology of the Church (English edition pp 70-73). It is of interest to note that this is not a section in its own right, but is included in the description of the ministry of the Holy Spirit in calling the Church into being and in 'calling, appointing and equipping believers to serve the Christian fellowship and be nourished by it'.

Is this an example of our wariness of anything that might be labelled 'churchiness'? True, our immutable 11 points are totally sufficient to satisfy our purpose of evangelism and soldier-making (indeed William Booth was 'conscious of no need for any theology in his service to the world but that which led men to the heart of Christ'). However, there is a place for the inclusion in our handbook of a Scripture-based statement of the purpose and pattern of our movement and the ministry of our soldiery and officers.

In O&R?

Here is given a definition of officership: 'The officers of the Salvation Army are men and women who:

- Have left ordinary pursuits and occupations.
- Have consecrated their lives to the service of God and the people.
- Have undergone a course of training.
- Are, unless retired, engaged in full-time service as leaders in the Army's ranks.'

(Part 1, Chapter 6, Section 1)

The significant point here is that officership is full-time and lifelong. The Conditions of Service outline this and the Covenant underlines it further. This is our equivalent to the 'indelible ministry' of the Church. Apart from this, *O&R* set out the qualities needed in an officer, describe the functions he or she performs, guide him or her in the most efficient ways to undertake the tasks and delineate the responsibilities of leadership and the principles which should be adhered to.

In our history?

It is said that our Founders were too busy making history to stop and write it down, but many of our clearest statements on the doctrine of the ministry and of officership in particular are found in the writings of William and Catherine Booth, General Bramwell Booth and Commissioner George Scott Railton.

The establishment of The Salvation Army, with its quasi-military structure, and the setting aside and commissioning of selected men and women as officers was not a haphazard improvisation, but Spirit-guided and Scripture-founded. There was a 'holy liberty', a flexibility, a freedom for the Spirit to move. The Founder's criteria were twofold:

1. Does it work?
2. Is it scriptural?

There was no confusion in the mind of William Booth about the fact that the Army was a part of the Church as much as any other denomination. As early as 1882, when the Church of England, impressed

A Theology of Officership

by The Salvation Army's success in soul winning with the masses, proposed union of the Army with that church, the Founder saw a divine purpose in our distinctive form of organisation, and could claim equal status for officers with the ordained clergy. He had overcome 'his ecclesiastical prejudice, the haunting sense of the minister's superiority and separateness', and could say in 1894:

The Salvation Army is not inferior in spiritual character to any organisation in existence... We are, I consider, equal in every way and anywhere to any other Christian organisation on the face of the earth in:

- *Spiritual authority.*
- *Spiritual intelligence.*
- *Spiritual function.*

We hold 'the keys' as truly as any church in existence.

And note, this included women officers, a deep point of division with the bishops. Catherine Booth's writings, particularly the address on 'The Salvation Army and its Relation to the Churches', reveal the conviction that The Salvation Army's style of organisation and ministry was truly apostolic, claiming for the Army a greater likeness to the Early Church than had been evident in any other group in Church history.

It was left to General Bramwell Booth to state most clearly the theology of the Church and the ministry as it related to the Army and officership. Stating that there is no 'blueprint' in Scripture for any particular form of church organisation and ministry, he drew attention to Christ's silence on the matter and the freedom he gave to his followers to adopt such forms and methods, under the guidance of the Holy Spirit, as would be 'wisest and appropriate'. As he so succinctly put it, 'Other rules would be appropriate to other times.'

He spells it out so clearly in pages 65-67 of *Echoes and Memories*[161] to which I would draw your attention, and from which I would quote this all too brief extract:

There is one Church of this, the Great Church of the Living God, we claim and have ever claimed, that we of The Salvation Army are

> *an integral part and element – a living fruit-bearing branch of the True Vine.*
>
> *No one who knows the Army can study the story of our Lord's selecting and calling the Twelve without being struck with the similarity in many respects – I say this with reverence – of our methods with his.*
>
> *We believe also that our system…is as truly and fully in harmony with the spirit set forth and the principles laid down by Jesus Christ and his Apostles as those which have been adopted by our brethren of other times and of other folds.*
>
> *And our officers are, equally with them, ministers in the Church of God…endowed by his grace, assured by his guidance, confirmed by his word, and commissioned by the Holy Spirit to represent him to the world.*

The exhilarating chapter, 'How the Buttons Came Off', gives a thrilling and inspiring account of the freedom in the Spirit, which enabled the Army to break free from the traditional views of the past in the system of government, in methods of worship and witness and in the commissioning of men and women to the ministry. It was a break with tradition, but not with Scripture!

In Scripture?

This leads us on to the source of our theology of officership – the Scriptures themselves. As stated, developments, innovations and changes from the traditional ordained ministry introduced by the Army were not merely the result of the pressures of our explosive growth and expansion, not merely interim measures or even eye-catching recruitment methods. All 'adaptation of measures' whether in method or ministry was in response to the Spirit's leading and founded in New Testament teaching.

In such an august company of training principals, all experts in theology, I wouldn't presume to deal with the subject of the doctrine of the ministry in Scripture and in the history of the Church. However, I thought we could seek to discover how the spirit of ministry in the New

Testament has given us the pattern for our officership:

1. It is modelled on Christ's ministry

'For even the Son of Man did not come to be served, but to serve, and to give his life as a ransom for many' (Mark 10:45).

The ministry of:
- Service or servanthood (to Christ and to the people).
- Reconciliation: '...entrusting to us the message of reconciliation' (2 Corinthians 5:19 *RSV*).

2. It is an apostolic ministry

Not apostolic in the ecclesiastical sense, but in the *spirit* of the Acts of the Apostles. The officer responds and is faithful to the divine compulsion to apostolic witness, leading to the transformation of the lives of people. An officer is 'commissioned', as were the apostles, to communicate to the world the gospel of Jesus Christ.

In *Called Out*,[162] Catherine Booth said: 'Whether our officers can claim apostleship in the estimation of the Church or not, they can certainly say with Paul: "If I be not an apostle unto others, yet doubtless I am to you: for the seal of mine apostleship are ye in the Lord"' (1 Corinthians 9:2 *KJV*).

3. We believe that all are called to the ministry

We believe in the priesthood of all believers, the ministry of the whole Church. This is in keeping with New Testament teaching as exemplified by the Early Church. The Salvation Army has never set up a two-tier structure – a professional priesthood and the laity. We have no dividing line between officers and soldiers; officers have no monopoly of the ministry; it is a shared ministry.

Like any human community, the Church – the Army – requires a focus of leadership and unity, and this the Holy Spirit provides in the call to full-time service for some. These leaders are needed to 'equip his people for works of service, so that the Body of Christ may be built up' (Ephesians 4:12).[163]

This leadership takes various patterns according to the needs of the people we serve. Hence the varieties of images – as evangelist, shepherd, teacher, ambassador, steward, examples in holiness and compassion. Officers may fill one or several of these roles...the corps officer more than most.

We must beware of developing a professional officer class. Rank does not imply superior status. 'Whoever wants to be first must be slave of all' (Mark 10:44).

The New Testament gives no authority for any kind of apostolic succession by the laying on of hands, nor for the setting apart of a special priesthood by ordination. This was a later development in the establishment of a professional ministry and a hierarchy. The threefold ministry in the New Testament of bishop-presbyter-deacon was no professional ministry, but concerned oversight within the Christian community.

The Church today is becoming increasingly aware of this ministry of all believers, which has been a foundation principle of The Salvation Army. An interesting example is found in the statement of the doctrine of the ministry agreed by the Anglican/Roman Catholic International Commission 1973.

Professor John Macquarrie [1919-2007], in drawing attention to the fundamental ministry of the whole Church and urging the active cooperation of the laity, illustrates this by mentioning The Salvation Army:

Its Founder, William Booth, could be regarded as a pioneer of 'secular' Christianity in its best sense, and one who long ago saw the need for the laity to assume a more active role in the industrialised modern world...I visualise the ministry of the laity in terms of practical service, having nothing ostensibly 'churchy' or 'religious' about it...and again The Salvation Army provides a good example.[164]

4. Women share in this ministry

Under the Spirit's guidance, The Salvation Army made an historic decision to give women an equal place in the ministry. In some ways, our history might imply that this was the result of a desperate, pragmatic action to meet the demands of a rapidly growing movement, short on manpower.

Women who could speak were encouraged to do so equally with men, thus by degrees, without preconceived arrangement, woman took for herself a place in the mission.

But this was not just an organisational expedient, for Catherine Booth had prepared the way for woman's place by her own deep convictions which had come through her study of the Scripture and through her obedience to the Holy Spirit's prompting. Her pamphlet, *Female Ministry*, is sufficient 'apology' for the whole position which the Army has claimed for and given to women in its ranks.

In this too, the Army gives a lead to the churches. The Army Mother in pinpointing the 'healthy effect the Army had on the churches', said:

> *The Army has taught them many valuable lessons. Amongst others, 'the universal compulsion of souls', 'Aggressive Christianity'* – *having coined the very term* – *'The employment of women', 'The utilisation of the laity', and so on. May we continue to do so.*[165]

Perhaps we could repeat, 'May we continue to do so.'

5. It is a flexible ministry

The Church of the New Testament and the ministry had a flexibility, even a 'healthy untidiness', and this allowed for developments, adaptations and changes to the overall pattern. This was in response to the Spirit's guidance in the face of specific needs. The Church is realising this afresh today, with its many new developments in ministry: worker-priests, industrial chaplaincies, team ministry, specialised ministries of many kinds.

The Army's approach to ministry has been characterised by this flexibility: ministries in music, in social service, and so on. More recently this has been manifest in the concept of full-time envoys and auxiliary-captains.

6. Officership is not a settled ministry

The Salvation Army was to be characterised by mobility. The Founder was 'dead against' forming another religious sect 'with its settled communities of good people sitting under a favourite preacher and keeping him among them so long as his popularity was maintained.' We were to be an Army on the move, always reaching out to those outside the Church and bringing them in to join a dynamic fighting force.

The principle of movement of officers by command, so that their appointments were to be in the hands of senior officers who, guided by God, would send them 'where they could most effectively advance the Kingdom' caused the Founder no little anxiety. Because of it, many officers were lost to us, of whom Railton wrote: 'They began to hanker after the rights, privileges, comforts, teaching and respectability of the Church.'

But the Founder felt divinely guided in the establishment of this principle. It was in line with the spirit of New Testament ministry, and aimed at providing a vital missionary force which would avoid the settled pattern that had stultified the mission of many churches.

Today, in spite of questions of consultation and the need for consolidation of ministry, this principle still stands. It is of interest to note this paragraph in a recent booklet [*The Role of the Corps Officer in the United States of America*]:

> *The corps officer receives his appointment from the appropriate administrative officer. Cooperation in this procedure is a prerequisite for officership. Each officer is bound to this procedure as long as he is an officer. There can be no exceptions. It must be retained if the Army is to maintain the strength of mobility which has contributed so much to its missionary success.*[166]

The basis of officership

I would like to set down for you a definition of officership, given by the late Commissioner Ernest Fewster which covers the basic points:

- The Salvation Army as part of the Church universal, has its own ordained ministry. Believing in the priesthood of all believers, those who are converted and have joined the ranks are commissioned to minister the good news of the gospel wherever they are.

- As in all denominations, some are called to make the ministry their vocation. So, in the Army, there are those who, because of the Divine impulse, leave all, commit themselves to God, become officers and like the apostles are willing to be directed to serve wherever he may choose.

- The officer is a leader, and it is to leadership of God's people

that he is called. This responsibility calls for:
1. A deep love for God and the people;
2. Dedication of heart, mind, body and spirit;
3. Willingness to serve as directed.

- Before an officer is commissioned, he must first be recommended as a suitable person on the local level. Having been satisfactorily recommended, his case is presented to the National Board. If accepted, he enters the training college, where he is taught the necessary techniques which, added to his native ability, will enable him to meet the tremendous demands of leadership.

We will look at the basic points:
- A divine calling – in both its active and passive strands.
- Acceptance – the Army tests the candidate's vocation; trains him or her; then tests the cadet's fitness for commissioning.
- Commissioning – a commission from God through the Army. 'A divine ordination.' Hence the demand for this to be an occasion of solemn dignity and due seriousness, investing the officer-to-be with the authority for his ministry. In the ceremonies connected with the commissioning of new officers it is interesting to note that, in many territories, the commissioning is quite separate from the appointments meeting.
- Full-time, lifelong service – following the pattern set in the New Testament, he or she fulfils his or her calling in a ministry that seeks to win men for Christ, serves and cares for them in Christ's name, and equips and enables fellow Salvationists to join in that ministry.

Conclusion

It is our responsibility to help young people see that there is no more worthy cause to which they could dedicate their lives.

Whilst it is important that the centrality of the divine call be emphasised, cadets in the training college should be made vitally aware of the scriptural principles on which officership itself rests, so that in those times when the splendour of the call may not be so bright, when the awareness of the call wanes, they will not easily be diverted from this ministry. Also whatever task they are called upon to do in the movement, they will see their role in the total work of the ministry; which is to enable the Army to fulfil its God-given task throughout the world.

In the training college, cadets need to be given a theological understanding of their officership and of our movement as part of the universal Church. In one way or another you no doubt seek to do this, but there is a need for a systematic study of the whole subject...apart from inspirational addresses regarding the kind of men and women officers should be.

Officership is a high calling, and those who train young people for it are most keenly and sensitively aware of its magnitude. They are accountable to God to help these young men and women comprehend the depth, the dimensions and the demands of this God-given service.

Who is equal to such a calling? We join Paul in the answer to his own question: 'Not that we are competent in ourselves to claim anything for ourselves, but our competence comes from God' (2 Corinthians 3:5).

Reading Guide

This serious stab at a theology of officership in 1974 collected the thinking of the previous century to provide a basis for understanding this fundamental form of Salvation Army leadership. In that sense it presaged Major Harold Hill's *Leadership in The Salvation Army: a Case Study in Clericalisation*,[167] a comprehensive treatment of the subject.

The then Colonel Burrows concludes one of her sections: 'Many need to realise that the officer's calling as "servant of all" does not mean he or she is to be the general handyman/woman for all.'

This clarification remains necessary in many instances, and not with soldiers only. There is a tension, of course. The servant leader must be always ready to serve and sacrifice and give and be interrupted; but the handyman/woman leader tends to carry expectations and burdens and routinize errands. The former is commendable (servant). The latter is lamentable (handyman/woman). The handyman/woman leader is leader in name only and cannot take followers very far.

We cannot develop maintainers and managers and helpers as officers, or our future is limited to the status quo. When there were great numbers of people responding to the calling to officership there were sufficient numbers of officers to do mundane tasks and routine jobs that did not require leadership abilities. They were humble servants. We could embrace anyone with a calling because the allowances were so small some were not required to lead. But in most territories today we recompense officers like leaders and we need leadership in return. And officers who routinely drive the bus to pick up people, or who routinely shovel the snow from the sidewalk and parking area are not using that time leading.

We need to create leaders with apostolic vision who don't settle with serving the small number of people in their first appointment but see that small group as the brigade to be trained and deployed to win the town for Jesus.

Colonel Burrows quotes a commission of the day that the 'master role' of the officer is evangelist. There are few officers today who would agree with an officer who always fills in 'occupation' entries of formal documents with the word 'evangelist'. But this term does not mean that the officer only evangelises. They should be training up others to evangelise as well.

Discussion Starters

1. How can you transition from 'handyman/woman for all' to 'servant of all' leader? And, to apostolic leader?

2. To what extent are you developing evangelist leaders? How can you do it more effectively?

3. Colonel Burrows addresses ordination and mentions General Orsborn's phrase 'ordination of the bleeding hands'. Does it still apply today? If not, how might it?

[161] Bramwell Booth, *Echoes and Memories*, 65-67, Hodder & Stoughton, London, 1925.
[162] Catherine Booth, *Called Out*, 40, IHQ, 1886.
[163] The original text runs: 'These leaders are needed to "coordinate the Spirit-given diversity of his people, to equip them to be ministers also and to share in the mission of evangelism, and to lead them on to maturity" (Ephesians 4:11-12).'
[164] John Macquarrie, *Principles of Christian Theology*, 376, SCM Press, Norwich, 2003.
[165] Catherine Booth, *The Salvation Army in Relation to the Church and State and Other Addresses*, 73, S.W. Partridge, London, 1883.
[166] *The Role of the Corps Officer in the United States of America*, 17, The Salvation Army, 1972.
[167] Harold Hill, *Leadership in The Salvation Army: a Case Study in Clericalisation*, Paternoster Press, London, 2006.

Chapter 13
Cross-cultural Training
by Captain Clive Adams
International Conference for Training Principals 2001

Introduction

HORSES for courses – to me, this phrase not only presents a layman's synopsis of the fundamental principle behind cross-cultural ministry but also, possibly, a principle for cross-cultural training. If the focus of all our training is preparation for leadership and ministry, cross-cultural training is a subject where the differences from one territory to the next must be taken into consideration. The breadth and depth by which the subject is addressed in any training system should be determined by the extent to which cross-cultural ministry is practised and/or necessary in a particular area.

The questions I would pose are:

1. What do we understand by the term 'cross-cultural ministry'? I believe that by considering the first question we will be laying a foundation upon which the subject before us can be addressed.

2. What does cross-cultural ministry mean? The term can be as broad or narrow as you like because 'culture' means everything – from that which distinguishes an occidental from an oriental or an African from an Indian, to the difference between someone who listens to heavy metal music and someone who pines for the Beatles.

Webster [*Merriam-Webster's Dictionary*] defines culture as, among other things: 'the set of shared attitudes, values, goals and practices that characterises a group.'

Therefore culture is definable by such variables as one's world view, customs, age, prejudices, belief or philosophy, education, nationality or tribal affiliation, language or group. Crossing the city from one corps to another can be a cross-cultural experience.

For the purposes of this paper, we will be considering three aspects of cross-cultural training:
1. The principle.
2. The programme.
3. The practice of.

The principle of cross-cultural training

If our training has as its objective equipping for ministry, then the principle of the one must be similar to the principle of the other. That principle can be stated as: 'Horses for courses'.

This principle of cross-cultural ministry is encapsulated in Paul's chameleon-like adaptation described in 1 Corinthians 9:19-22: 'Though I am free and belong to no one, I have made myself a slave to everyone, to win as many as possible. To the Jews I became like a Jew, to win the Jews. To those under the law I became like one under the law (though I myself am not under the law), so as to win those under the law. To those not having the law I became like one not having the law (though I am not free from God's law but am under Christ's law), so as to win those not having the law. To the weak I became weak, to win the weak. I have become all things to all people so that by all possible means I might save some.'

Warren Wiersbe comments on this passage as follows:

Though Paul enjoyed liberty as a worker, he willingly made himself the servant of all men that he might win them to Christ. This does not mean that Paul followed the worldly slogan, 'When in Rome, do as the Romans do.' That would be compromise rooted in fear. Paul's attitude was based on love, not fear. He was not lowering his standards; rather, he was laying aside his personal privileges. It was not hypocrisy, but sympathy: he tried to understand those who needed Christ and enter into their experiences. 'All things to all men' (v 22) simply means the wonderful ability of accommodating ourselves to others, understanding them and seeking to lead them into the knowledge of Christ. Paul was no tactless 'bull in a china shop' who used the same approach on all he met. Rather, he used tact to get contact; he willingly sacrificed his own privileges to win the lost.[168]

Frederick Booth-Tucker in India understood this principle as he paved the way for a revolutionary alternative to the 'pith helmet mentality' which had infected so much missionary endeavour elsewhere. That mentality had conducted cross-cultural ministry through reproducing Little Englands/final bastions of Westernism by transporting the things and thoughts of home to the mission field. These isolated the preachers from their prospects to the extent that those receiving ministry could not distinguish between culture and Christianity, so that getting saved meant wearing trousers and speaking 'Inglis'.

Booth-Tucker proved that when you live among the people as one of them, understanding and empathising with their everyday lives, your 'street cred' is much higher than if you live apart and maintain a separate lifestyle which does not touch their lives. He understood, way ahead of his time, that people turn away from the gospel not because they reject Christ or his call to repentance, but because some zealot for 'Christian tradition' has demanded adherence to 'Christian cultural norms'. Jesus did not die for Muslims to eat pork, or natives to wear trousers – or Salvation Army brass bands to stand on a hill, deep in rural Zululand, playing Larsson's tunes. Sue Rinaldi – a British gospel singer – is quoted as saying: 'It is not Jesus being rejected but the [cultural] wrapper in which he is placed.' And this includes deciding what is 'Army' and what is not. Horses for courses.

How can we inculcate this principle of adaptation into officers' attitudes when they cross cultures in ministry? I believe that this principle can be grasped by the following aspects of training:

- Interpretation: knowing the Scriptures. Studying the Old Testament to discover what was Hebrew culture and what was God's law. Studying the New Testament to discover what is Christian and what is culture.
- Investigation: knowing yourself. Learning about your personality and culture.

- Identification: I become all things to all people. Living among the people.
- Investigation: knowing them. Learning about the culture of the people. Learning about the culture from the people.
- Incarnation: the messenger is the message. Living out the message before the people.

It is not about the transference of facts, but the transformation of lives. Geir Engoy, Cross-cultural Ministries Secretary in the USA Western Territory, in identifying these points, quotes Eugene Nida, who says: 'All divine communication (read "cross-cultural ministry") is essentially incarnational, for it comes, not only in words, but in life. Even if a truth is given only in words, it has no real validity until it has been translated into life.'

The programme for cross-cultural training

The curriculum for this subject needs to be tailored around the specific outcomes you have set according to the requirements of the learner and/or the territory. Your course content would differ greatly if your focus was 'the youth subculture of the inner cities of eastern USA' or if you were preparing a Swiss leader to work in Papua New Guinea. I have listed some of the issues that could be important in equipping learners for cross-cultural ministry:

- Church planting models/evangelism methods.
- Conflict management DiSC programme (or the like).
- English (read 'Spanish/French…' and so on) as a second language.
- Interpersonal skills.
- Music.
- Practical issues.
- Spiritual warfare.
- Team ministry.
- Theory.

The practice of cross-cultural training

The most significant cross-cultural training occurs when learners are placed into, or exposed to, a new culture. Learners experience cross-cultural situations – often in a crisis – in a way that cannot be explained in a class. They often learn hard lessons through their own mistakes, which reside deeper than facts shared on an overhead projector.

The practical aspect of cross-cultural training can occur in several ways:
- Communal living of mixed cultures.
- Experience in cross-cultural ministry in field training and campaigns.
- Learning the basics in regard to primary health care and community service (visiting areas).
- Second-language courses.
- Contextualising other subjects, such as doctrine (e.g. by comparing world views) and principles and procedures (e.g. by highlighting different cultural practices for various ceremonies).

Reading Guide

This subject is relevant for all of us, whether or not we are serving in countries overseas. The mixture of cultures and subcultures in most places requires of us some engagement with the teaching here provided. 'Horses for courses' is the principle ('all things to all people so that by all possible means I might save some').

We are challenged to follow the steps of interpretation, investigation, identification, investigation (again) and incarnation strategically. So, the challenge in training leaders is to train them to train others who will progress through this exercise to optimise the great commission impact on their fronts.

Captain [now Commissioner] Adams provides these questions to stimulate application.

Discussion Starters

1. Is it reasonable to assume that, unlike foundational subjects (such as theology, biblical studies, church history) where the content and intensity of study has generally agreed parameters, the priority given to cross-cultural training should be at territorial

discretion? Robin Markowitz talks about defining a 'canon of academic knowledge'; does cross-cultural training merit a place in a 'canon for officer-training'? Is cross-cultural training an option or an imperative depending on the degree to which cross-cultural ministry is an issue in any geographical areas of the Army?

2. Should cross-cultural training be offered as a specific course exclusively for those being considered for cross-cultural ministry?

3. Are there principles of cross-cultural ministry that have general application for ministry regardless of whether cultures are being crossed or not? If so, is it accurate to label such training as 'cross-cultural training' when, in effect, it is general training for ministry?

4. Are cross-cultural training principles transferable? If I learn principles in preparation for reinforcement service (Western vs. developing world), could these apply to an appointment as a divisional youth worker (modernism vs. postmodernism)?

---

[168] Warren Wiersbe, Expository Outlines on the New Testament, David C. Cook, Colorado Springs, CO, 1992.

Chapter 14
Spiritual Leadership in The Salvation Army
by Dr Jonathan S. Raymond
International Conference for Training Principals 2001

WE live in a time of remarkable transition. We have left the industrial age and are entering some other unnamed age for which we have not yet formed an appropriate label. No matter how we manage to describe it – post-industrial, postmodern, the space age, the information age – for sure it will not be characterised as 'same old, same old'. The future will not be more of the same. Our ideas of leadership are changing with the times and this includes how we think about spiritual leaders as well. The days may be gone when we think of spiritual leaders as super heroes of the faith who create dramatic change and occasion a worshipful following. New metaphors and paradigms for leadership are emerging and changing how we think of leaders, and in particular spiritual leaders.

I wish to suggest five propositional truths regarding spiritual leadership in The Salvation Army. These five propositions reflect neither a comprehensive understanding of the topic nor one without its flaws and shortcomings. These five propositional truths about spiritual leadership in The Salvation Army emerge in my remarks to you today as follows:

1. Personal holiness in the context of a full salvation is spiritual leadership's essential character.

2. Social holiness in the context of Christian community is spiritual leadership's calling.

3. Ecological responsiveness is spiritual leadership's task orientation.

4. Responsiveness to a suffering world completes it.

5. A faith-based certainty (assurance) about identity and mission empowers spiritual leadership as partnership with the divine.

Personal holiness

A spiritual leader in The Salvation Army lives out the theology of the Army. Ours is a relational theology of grace and restoration. An orthodox understanding of our salvation is that it is far more than a forensic, legal moment of justification by faith in which we are saved from the uttermost of sin. Indeed, our salvation is truly a restoration to Christlikeness and therefore to personal holiness. Whether as a commissioner or a newly commissioned local officer, Salvation Army spiritual leadership seeks firstly to mature and grow by faith in holiness, and secondly to experience purity of heart. With the words of the Psalmist, the spiritual leader pleads:

Create in me a pure heart, O God,
and renew a steadfast spirit within me.
Do not cast me from your presence
or take your Holy Spirit from me.
Restore to me the joy of your salvation
and grant me a willing spirit, to sustain me.
(Psalm 51:10-12).

As we may say of all humankind, Salvationists are a predestined people. We are predestined to holiness. It is God's plan from the beginning that all persons everywhere live as the *Imago Dei*, the Image of God. This was God's plan and remains his plan for our lives, not in the 'sweet by and by' but now, for all people at all times. This is our destiny. Anything else and anything less is not an option. God does not offer a 'plan B'. The spiritual leader in The Salvation Army embraces his or her destiny. They respond to the call to holiness and are cleansed and equipped to serve with Christ to bring to all others the good news of our destiny, of a full salvation, of restoration. As songwriters Alfred and Bentley Ackley have written:

'Til the whole world knows,
'Til the whole world knows...

Spiritual leaders in The Salvation Army understand holiness to be a matter of both maturity and purity along a continuum of God's grace.

The words from the chorus of another old Army song speak of the continuum of God's grace and go like this:

Jesus is mighty to save!
Jesus is mighty to save!
From the uttermost [of sin], *to the uttermost* [of Christlikeness],
Mighty to save!
(*SASB* 249)

General Frederick Coutts, in *The Call To Holiness*,[169] underscores the importance of an unfolding, maturing, increasingly intimate holiness experience when he speaks of Christian perfection, and quotes three verses:

1. Philippians 3:15: 'All of us, then, who are mature should take such a view of things.'
2. Ephesians 4:13: 'until we all…become mature.'
3. Hebrews 6:1: 'Let us…go on to maturity' (*NIV 1984*).

For some Salvationists, General Coutts's emphasis on holiness as process is much preferred over Samuel Logan Brengle's[170] strong orientation to holiness as a crisis experience. A close reading of Coutts and Brengle reveals their mutual focus on both process and crisis, though emphases may differ. We find this discussion of process or crisis alive and carried on in contemporary [2001] Wesleyan scholarship. Randy Maddox, author of *Responsible Grace*,[171] proposed more emphatically than Coutts that holiness is a matter of process and daily handling responsibly the grace God gives us. Maddox bases his position on his interpretation of John Wesley's writings on holiness as influenced by Eastern Orthodoxy and by the writings of the Early Church fathers. In contrast to Maddox's position on holiness as process is Wesleyan scholar, Kenneth Collins, in his work *The Scripture Way of Salvation*[172] and subsequent writings. Collins attempts to correct Maddox's discounting of Moravian and Lutheran influences on Wesley which emphasise a tradition of holiness as crisis.

For the spiritual leader in The Salvation Army I wish to propose a 'juxtaposynthesis' of process and crisis to say that personal holiness is both and more. You intuitively know and experience juxtaposyntheses. When two colours, blue and yellow, are laid side by side – that is, juxtaposed to each other – green emerges as a synthesis. When we add curry and hot pepper to sweet potato soup, a culinary synthesis takes place, especially with a little lime juice added. Or when the *Pieta*, Mary holding the crucified Christ in her arms, is decorated with coloured Christmas lights, we may reflect on the vulgarities of Christmas commercialism. With God's wonderful gift of our minds, we experience juxtaposyntheses, in which the whole is truly greater than the sum of its parts.

I believe that holiness is our destiny. I believe it is a juxtaposynthesis of process and crisis, of Coutts and Brengle, of Maddox and Collins. I believe John Bunyan got it right in the first place in his *The Pilgrim's Progress*. Personal holiness is sustained intimacy as both journey and encounter. Throughout the journey there are opportunities for qualitatively different processes and encounters. Not all encounters are crises of cleansing. Some encounters are of healing and reconciliation, some of cleansing, while others are of compassion. A consequence of faithfully continuing the journey with Christ, walking in the light of God and in the Spirit, is that by God's grace, and through encounters with his grace, we grow and mature in our likeness to Christ.

Another consequence is that we encounter Christ and he encounters us along the pathway – the pathway of duty if you will – of obedience. This was Gideon's experience in the book of Judges. Gideon passed through a series of encounters with God, of opportunities with risks, opportunities for obedience, and God's responses to Gideon's obedience led to strengthened faith, followed by further encounters. Gideon experienced an interactive, dynamic relationship of deepening intimacy with God through the journey. This too was the learner's experience with Jesus. It was the Apostle Paul's as well. The Founder, William Booth, captured the essence of the journey and its encounters when he penned Salvation Army doctrines 9 and 10:

We believe that continuance in a state of salvation depends upon continued obedient faith in Christ.

We believe that it is the privilege of all believers to be wholly sanctified, and that their whole spirit and soul and body may be preserved blameless unto the coming of our Lord Jesus Christ.

Continuing in a state of salvation is continuing the salvation journey along the pathway of restoration to holiness and service. How the journey goes, and what we encounter along the way, depends upon our continual obedient faith in Christ.

Acts 2:42 says the Early Church grew as they continually devoted themselves to the means of grace – good teaching, fellowship, the breaking of bread, and prayer. These means of grace were God's means of being present and revealing himself. They promoted a maturing of their faith. It was a sustained, obedient faith, practising together in community the presence of Christ in the Christian life. It remains so today. It is living the life, stepping out each day into a journey of continual consecration. What the spiritual leader consecrates, God sanctifies wholly, completely, entirely and makes holy, set apart for him and with him in service.

Another way of thinking about personal holiness as journey and encounter for the spiritual leader in The Salvation Army is that each new day Jesus meets us at our heart's door. He is not there knocking to come in. Rather, he is there at the door on the inside inviting us to go out with him into his life to encounter his plan for the day and to encounter those he loves and those he plans to serve throughout the day in partnership with us. He invites us to journey with him and to meet and greet, and serve others. Together with Christ and with others, the spiritual leader provides leadership that creates the conditions for others to journey as well, and in so doing, they experience restoration to holiness.

This is the heart of spiritual leadership – responding to the personal call to walk with Jesus each day in holiness through journeys and encounters, and to bring others along as well.

Social holiness

Spiritual leaders who contribute to creating the conditions for others' journeys, encounters, and restoration, do so as they are immersed in social holiness. John Wesley was known for saying 'The gospel of Christ knows of no religion but social, no holiness but social holiness.'[173] Brengle and Coutts agreed. We engage a relational theology of grace modelled after our Lord and the Trinity – the Three in One relationally integrated yet distinct from one another – 'Three persons in the Godhead undivided in essence', in communion with each other and by grace in communion with the spiritual leader. The Trinity models community and the social life of God and God's people.

Modelling after the Holy Spirit who is the Paraclete, spiritual leaders, then, seek out others and come alongside. The Paraclete draws close, is a presence, brings comfort and guidance, and remains available as a companion for the journey. Social holiness is not a euphemism for The Salvation Army's social services, though we would pray that all Army social services were settings of social holiness. Perhaps a more powerful, more succinct understanding of social holiness in spiritual leadership is the social ecology of holiness and restoration. In Acts 2:42, as the Early Church continually devoted itself to the means of grace, there must have been spiritual leaders who created, promoted and fostered the conditions for new Christians' journey, growth, and encounters. The conditions are often not only personal, but also social.

Colonel Phil Needham makes this point when he writes in *Word & Deed*[174] that holiness is not uni-directional. It does not just work in one direction. A holy people are not merely an aggregation of Spirit-filled individuals who achieve a critical mass of holiness. The spiritual ecology of Christian community represents the conditions within which the Holy Spirit moves and does its best work in the hearts of others. Spiritual leadership in the West may struggle with this idea of a social ecology of holiness and often fails to create the conditions for immersion, growth and encounter. This is because in the West we are shackled to a belief system that honours rugged individualism, personal striving, and cultish acts of hero worship. We love to think of holiness in John Wayne, Clint Eastwood and Bruce Willis (or Bruce Lee) terms.

Leadership, including spiritual leadership, particularly in the West, is defined as driving change.[175] It celebrates and idolises as a hero one who faces a crisis and makes those changes which resolve the crisis. This leads to one-way thinking, that if we can gather together enough holy individuals to establish critical mass, we will achieve social holiness of community. The opposite may actually be more the case. When the community of believers comes together as a people set apart in the presence of a holy God, holiness and restoration can and does follow. This was true in the life of the Early Church. This was true of the Methodist movement and its social transformational power in John Wesley's day. This was also true of The Salvation Army throughout the world in its beginnings.

Scripture reminds us: 'If my people, who are called by my name, will humble themselves and pray…' (2 Chronicles 7:14) and '"…I bound the whole house of Israel and the whole house of Judah to me," declares the Lord, "to be my people for my renown and praise and honour"' (Jeremiah 13:11 *NIV 1984*).

Spiritual leaders help others come together as a people to seek God's face, experience his presence, and know in whose presence they stand. Spiritual leaders create the conditions of immersion for others in the ecology of holiness found in relationship to God and to each other. Spiritual leadership promotes a social holiness that is lived out in community, in righteousness, and in social justice. They promote the conditions in which sanctification spills over into liberation. There is a direct tie between social holiness and social justice and the fulfilment of Scripture. 'And what does the Lord require of you? To act justly and to love mercy and to walk humbly with your God' (Micah 6:8).

The social-ecological nature of spiritual leadership

Leadership is traditionally viewed as having vision and driving change toward that vision. The spiritual leader jumps metaphorically into the driver's seat and manipulates the gears and wheels of heavy equipment to change the direction and speed of the machine we call the church or corps. This is a metaphor which is a vestige of the industrial age where machines and skilled operators reigned. But it is the wrong metaphor. Leading is not driving change by manipulating and operating heavy equipment, powerful and effective as such imagery may be.

A more powerful and more biblical metaphor is the leader as gardener. Is it of any consequence for our discussion that the God-man interface first took place in a garden? Scripture says that we are like a tree planted by a stream. In John chapter 15 (*NASB*), Jesus says of himself and of our relationship to him: 'I am the vine, you are the branches (v 5) and 'My Father is the vinedresser' (v 1).

Ecological metaphors are abundant. Rather than thinking of spiritual communities as a large machine to be driven somewhere, a more profound way is to think of them as 'communities of interest' which have a capacity to bring forth new realities, as does a well cared for garden. Gardening requires vision – an image of a desirable future – but it also requires intentional acts of sowing seeds, nurturing growth conditions, including pulling weeds, pruning, watering and regulating temperatures.

Spiritual leaders tend to their gardens even when it means their own self-denial. We read in Scripture that Greeks sought to speak with Jesus just before Passover and his journey to the Cross. There is no mention that Jesus ever actually spoke with them. Instead, Jesus says to his disciple Andrew: 'Very truly I tell you, unless a grain of wheat falls to the ground and dies, it remains only a single seed. But if it dies, it produces many seeds' (John 12:24).

Spiritual leaders in The Salvation Army must think, live, and die to self ecologically. They must be like the gardener promoting the conditions for the community to live and grow together in holiness, producing the fruit of the Spirit. No one ever commanded seeds to grow. No gardener stands over the seeds and shouts, 'Grow seeds, grow!' Instead, the gardener goes about his or her work – not controlling the seeds, but rather influencing the conditions under which the seeds will realise their potential, their destiny, God's design for their existence. When is the last time you thought of learners as seeds and the training system as a garden?

Spiritual leadership in the context of suffering humanity

In the provocative words of General John Gowans, The Salvation Army was invented to save souls, grow saints and serve suffering humanity. The Canada and Bermuda Territory has captured this statement in a lovely poster. The USA Southern Territory has reduced the statement further to an easily remembered three Ss: Souls, Saints, and Service. Such efficiency of words, however, may be achieved at a price of potentially forgetting who it is we are called to serve – suffering humanity.

Spiritual leadership does not forget! We must not forget, and we work so that others may remember. We remember a suffering world where:[176]

- Of children under the age of five, 32,000 die of preventable causes each day. That is more than 11 million preventable deaths each year. For every child who dies, two more live with significant mental and/or physical impairment.
- Some 140 million children are missing out on primary education each year to work at home, in the fields, in sweatshops, and on the streets.
- In Africa, Asia and East Europe 30 countries suffer from armed conflict in which 90 per cent of casualties are civilian.
- In Chechnya, 40 per cent of civilian casualties are children and in 1995 in Sarajevo one in four children was wounded by the armed conflict.
- One in five of the world's six billion people (1.2 billion) struggle to survive on an income of less than one dollar a day.
- More than 50 per cent of the world's population is under the age of 25.
- One billion of the world's young people are teenagers deciding whether to smoke, drink alcohol, experiment with drugs or have their first sexual encounter. These are high-risk years with lifelong consequences.
- Half of all HIV/Aids cases occur among young people under the age of 25.
- In the African continent, 2.5 million people are infected with Aids and 95 per cent don't know it. Only 20,000 Africans are receiving drugs for Aids.
- Thirty per cent of women in Latin America and 50-60 per cent in sub-Saharan Africa have their first child as teenagers.
- The poor account for 80 per cent of the world's youth.

Europe is filled with young refugees, Africa with child soldiers, Latin America with street children, and Asia with child labourers, while North America's children are overweight, overly entertained and numbed by affluence.[177]

At no other time in modern history has such a large proportion of the world's human resources been so youthful. The world's population is now expanding by 90 million people a year – roughly the population of Mexico. Of the population growth forecast between 1990 and 2050, 97 per cent will be in developing countries. Of the 1.1 billion adolescents in the world today who are aged from 10 to 19 years, 913 million live in the world's poorest nations.

Employment opportunities will not keep pace with population growth. Between 1990 and 2010, North Africa's economically active population, for example, is expected to grow by 29 million, but only 5 million new jobs will be created during the same time. The gap between the world's 'haves' and 'have-nots' is widening. The share of global income of the poorest 20 per cent of the world's population has dropped from 2.3 per cent to 1.4 per cent since the late 1960s. The assets of just 358 people in the world are greater today than the combined annual income of 45 per cent (2.6 billion) of the world's people.

Add to this a litany of related issues that include racism, intentional female illiteracy, crime, violence, child prostitution, sexual abuse and exploitation and it brings us a deeper appreciation of the words of Jesus: 'Let the little children come to me' (Matthew 19:14); and Scripture which says: 'When he saw the crowds, he had compassion on them, because they were harassed and helpless, like sheep without a shepherd. Then he said to his disciples, "The harvest is plentiful but the workers are few. Ask the Lord of the harvest, therefore, to send out workers into his harvest field"' (Matthew 9:36-38).

We remember Jesus' fulfilment of Scripture from Isaiah when he said: 'The Spirit of the Lord is on me, because he has anointed me to proclaim good news to the poor. He has sent me to proclaim freedom for the prisoners and recovery of sight for the blind, to set the oppressed free, to proclaim the year of the Lord's favour' (Luke 4:18-19).

- Spiritual leadership sings General Albert Orsborn's words:
    Except I am moved with compassion,
    How dwelleth thy Spirit in me?
    (*SASB* 527)

- Spiritual leadership sees the connection between social holiness and social justice. It does not forget the poor, the disenfranchised, the marginalised, the despised, the oppressed, and the abused. It does not suffer amnesia nor is it distracted by the entertainment cultures of affluence and materialism.
- Spiritual leadership, from commissioners to commissioned local officers, advocates for the poor, washes their feet, and works for their redemption, restoration, and liberation. Spiritual leadership identifies with Jesus by identifying with the poor, remembering Christ's words: 'whatever you did for one of the least of these brothers and sisters of mine, you did for me' (Matthew 25:40).
- Spiritual leadership identifies with the Scripture verse in Isaiah 49:6 – 'It is too small a thing for you to be my servant to restore the tribes of Jacob and bring back those of Israel I have kept. I will also make you a light for the Gentiles, that my salvation may reach to the ends of the earth.'
- Spiritual leadership sees that it is too small a thing to just stop at personal holiness and that social-ecological holiness must be expressed in social justice, that the great commandment is expressed in the great commission, that the only thing that truly counts is faith expressing itself in love actively identifying with a needy, suffering world.

Identity and mission

Spiritual leadership in The Salvation Army finds its identity and mission in the midst of God's grace and salvation. It is central to our Wesleyan distinctive that as we practise various means of grace, or, in Randy Maddox's terms, as we respond to the grace God gives us, we come to be increasingly aware of God's presence and of his identity. It is in the context of an increased awareness of God's presence, and an understanding of his identity, that faith grows and matures. This is why Jesus says: 'Abide with me! Walk with me! Journey with me!' It is in his presence and by seeing his identity as he reveals himself to us that we discover our identity – who we are in Christ and who we were and would be outside of an intimate relationship with Christ.

And in his presence, taking on our unique expression of his identity, we too have a presence in this world. Christ has a presence through us. From his presence and identity in us, by his grace given and received, we have a new identity and a profound presence in the world. We are salt and light, preserving, illuminating and restoring that which was lost. This is the story of the woman at the well, who one day in Christ's presence and by the revelation of his identity, encountered Jesus and became a transformed, restored presence in her village.

Spiritual leadership in The Salvation Army seeks God's presence, identifies completely with Jesus Christ, seeks the Holy Spirit's constant infilling and actively seeks to be a Spirit-filled presence in the world, co-labouring with Christ for his glory.

Identity reflects being. Mission is doing. Mission is always informed by identity as the doing always comes out of being. Spiritual leaders attend to their being – being in Christ, being holy as he is holy, being responsible to handle the grace God gives them and then to do mission and ministry. Out of this grounding in being like Jesus, spiritual leaders help others to fulfil their destiny of restoration to Christlikeness, and to come also to be co-labourers with Jesus, serving him and others.

You have a very high privilege, by the grace of God, to prepare spiritual leaders for The Salvation Army in the form of learners who as spiritual leaders will go on to prepare others. It is a most sacred trust. With Christ Jesus, you are up to the task as you live out our ninth doctrine remembering the apostle Paul's words to the Philippians: 'Continue to work out your salvation with fear and trembling, for it is God who works in you to will and to act in order to fulfil his good purpose' (Philippians 2:12-13) and John Wesley's favourite Scripture verse: 'The only thing that counts is faith expressing itself through love' (Galatians 5:6).

God bless all Salvation Army training principals!

Reading Guide/Discussion Starters

Dr Raymond's five propositions regarding spiritual leadership in The

Salvation Army are worth some discussion:

1. Personal holiness in the context of a full salvation is spiritual leadership's essential character.

It is an expectation and requirement. Major Geoff Webb has asserted that sanctification is a theological necessity for Wesleyans (such as us). Dr Raymond confidently affirms that from the newest local officer to the most mature commissioner, this is the standard. Where do you stand on this issue? It is an apostolic principle that you can only give what you have (think of Peter with no gold but the power to heal lame people). So, if you are going to train leaders to lead others into holiness, your response to this question is crucial to your leader-training effectiveness.[178]

2. Social holiness in the context of Christian community is spiritual leadership's calling.

This is an important development from the last generation and the evangelical infatuation with all things personal and individual (e.g. personal relationship with Jesus; Jesus as your personal Saviour). Raymond asserts that a spiritual leader should cultivate social holiness in the context of Christian community. How can you intentionally train learners to lead toward these ends?

3. Ecological responsiveness is spiritual leadership's task orientation.

Here's a new metaphor. No more 'driver's seat' analogies, if this catches on. We'll all be growing tomatoes in the community garden and developing teaching illustrations on leadership. How does this metaphor sit with you? What are its strengths and limitations?

4. Responsiveness to a suffering world completes it.

We are challenged by General John Gowans to serve suffering humanity. It is an effective means of accomplishing our mission to win the world for Jesus. It is also a (super)natural overflow of Christ's compassion filling us when we experience personal holiness. How can we authentically engage the suffering in the name and power of Jesus toward strategic great commission ends? What are the dynamics we must consider?

5. A faith-based certainty (assurance) about identity and mission empowers spiritual leadership as partnership with the divine.

Hallelujah! This has been implicit through the book. Dr Raymond spells it out here. Knowing who we are and what we are assigned to accomplish empowers us to co-labour with God toward the end of winning the world for Jesus. How can we inculcate this in learners who will inevitably be leading in situations requiring divine partnership and empowerment?

---

[169] Frederick L. Coutts, *The Call To Holiness*, SP&S, London, 1957. (See also Wayne Pritchett, 'General Frederick Coutts and the Doctrine of Holiness,' 49-64, in *Word & Deed*, Fall 1998, The Salvation Army, USA National Publications, Alexandria, VA.

[170] David Rightmire, 'Samuel Logan Brengle and the Development of Salvation Army Pneumatology', 29-48, in *Word & Deed*, ibid.

[171] Randy L. Maddox, *Responsible Grace: John Wesley's Practical Theology*, Abingdon Press, Nashville, TN, 1994.

[172] Kenneth J. Collins, *The Scripture Way of Salvation: The Heart of John Wesley's Theology*, Abingdon Press, ibid, 1997.

[173] *The Works of the Rev. John Wesley*, 593, Carlton & Porter, New York, NY, 1856.

[174] Phil Needham, 'Integrating Holiness and Community: The Task of an Evolving Salvation Army', 5-20, in *Word & Deed*, Fall 2000, ibid.

[175] Peter M. Senge, 'Leadership in Living Organizations,' in *Leading Beyond the Walls*, (Frances Hesselbein, Marshall Goldsmith, and Iain Somerville, eds.), Jossey-Boss Inc, Wiley, San Francisco, CA, 1999.

[176] Statistics and data like those noted in the text of this paper are readily available in a diversity of reports and publications from international agencies and organisations such as UNICEF, World Health Organisation, World Bank and International Red Cross/Crescent. The information presented in this paper gleans from several sources. While the specific data and findings may change in precision from study to study and from year to year, the overall message of human suffering and need does not change.

[177] For an excellent review of the relationship of holiness to social justice, see Theodore Runyon, *Sanctification & Liberation: Liberation Theologies in Light of the Wesleyan Tradition*, Abingdon Press, ibid, 1981.

[178] For more on this subject see Geoff Webb, Rowan Castle and Stephen Court, *Holiness Incorporated: Living and Working Beyond Corporate Integrity*, Salvo Publishing, The Salvation Army Australia Southern Territory, Blackburn, Victoria, 2009.

Chapter 15
Head, Hands and Heart – The Training of Salvation Army Officers (Leaders)
by General Eva Burrows (Retired)

TRAINING of Salvation Army leaders is the key to the effectiveness and growth of The Salvation Army. That's not an exaggeration. General Frederick Coutts declared: 'The quality of The Salvation Army depends on the quality of its officers.' This is not a denigration of Salvationist soldiery, but we must have a quality of leadership that inspires, enthuses and intelligently applies the principles that underpin this movement. That's why training and preparation for officership and leadership is crucial.

General Clarence Wiseman said: 'Salvation Army officers might be described as idealists without illusions. Even when their heads are in Heaven, they are required to keep both feet firmly planted on the ground.' That is why our college is not a university or theological college; much more than academic training in knowledge and intellectual skills is required. It is more like God's military academy, turning out leaders to lead God's Army in the fight against evil, injustice, poverty, suffering and despair with aggressive evangelism, mobilised for action in a world of human need, prepared for practical and effective spiritual warfare.

Human nature being what it is, some studious learners may prefer the ivory tower to the place of action; others are inclined to look at theoretical textbooks as obstacles to getting on with the job. So the training system has to effect a holy juxtaposition of the two.

Training officers have the responsibility of training in three key areas:
1. Head.
2. Hands.
3. Heart.

With the head

Conscientious study of the truth of Christian faith; digging deep into the Bible, God's Word. 'To give an answer to everyone who asks you to give the reason for the hope that you have' (1 Peter 3:15).

Study of humanity – human relationships; what makes people tick; why people behave as they do, especially in researching social problems. Not just naïve do-gooders, for example: looking into the deeper causes as to why a man is drinking himself to death; why loneliness is one of the chief social diseases of today; why a young boy vandalises other people's property; why one marriage in two ends in divorce; how to challenge the government; how to be an advocate for the poor; how to articulate for those who can't speak up for themselves.

Study how to communicate effectively; to get the message across to the listener, clear and plain; use of modern technology in communication and how to handle the media. But not just analyse academically. Learners need to see what they can do about it. William Booth: 'Go and do something!'

With the hands

Learning through practical experience; reaching out to people where they hurt, with compassion, sympathy and love.

Jesus used his hands a lot, not just as a carpenter, but in ministry. Handing out food to the hungry, cooking breakfast for his learners, touching the eyes of the blind, lifting up the leper, or washing the learners' dirty feet with the hands of God. They must learn to serve with loving hands, no task too lowly.

Leaders serve in a Christlike way with their hands: drying the tears of an abused child; comforting a lonely old man who is facing death with fear; cleaning up after a drunken woman; teaching a young offender the joy of using a tool constructively. No task too humble; no person too low to be served.

With the heart

Bramwell Booth said: 'Heart power is the great power. It is the highest wisdom, the noblest wealth. In the teaching of Christ to his learners, it is supreme.' Love to God first, then love for the people. Loving without limit. Loving as Christ loved. Loving even when love is spurned or met with ingratitude or resentment. Though leaders may understand about the background and causes of human problems and suffering, it will mean little unless they serve out of love. Their training must ensure that they understand this.

A government social worker told a cadet on practical social training: 'Don't let yourself get too fond of these people, or you won't be able to bear it.' But that is what a Salvation Army leader is called to do…to get fond of people. Sharing the compassion of Christ, who won by love and not coercion.

We have more to offer than a food voucher, a bed for the night, money for the fuel bill, or even a listening ear. Love is the plus of a Salvation Army leader's caring concern for people.

Conclusion

We need to train leaders who serve with head, hands and heart and to adapt a well known Bible verse (1 Corinthians 13:13), 'the greatest of these is the heart'.

Reading Guide

With head, hands and heart, General Burrows lays out the requirements of Salvation Army leadership. If we focus on the head only, we might create leaders who craft wonderful philosophies of ministry and well researched strategic plans and deep teaching, but do little of spiritual consequence. If we focus on the hands only, we could end up with leaders who might do, but might not do, what God wants them to do. And if we focus on heart only, we are vulnerable to developing loving and kind people who get nothing done. One maxim regarding the hiring of staff suggests that you bring people on board who love God, love people and are able to get things done. We want leaders with strengths in each of these areas.

So it is essential that we train to those ends. We must intentionally develop each of these areas. Salvation Army leadership training has three components: education, field and spiritual. These exactly match head, hands and heart.

Nothing spiritual is learned except by revelation. So, while teaching and research can be helpful in this area, we must provide the environment and cultivate experiences of spiritual revelation and experimentation. Reading books of the saints can only help so much. Learning about the great warriors of the past has limited value. But investing a few hours at a time in prayer cannot be matched. The same principle applies to spiritual warfare, the prophetic and spiritual gifts. Engagement trumps classroom learning. Exercise beats research.

This continues into field training. The fellowship is in the fight. It will be beneficial for you to do some fighting alongside your learners so they can see how you do it. Then they can try it themselves. At this point they will be in a better position to train others.

Finally, education. It can bolster the spiritual and field components. But it often becomes the default emphasis for leader training. We must always be wary of the inclination to fall back on the classroom model of training.

We need all three components: head, hands and heart; education, field and spiritual.

Discussion Starters

1. Does your training include head and hands and heart? How can you correct any imbalances in emphasis?

2. Are you intentional in providing opportunities for learners to experience what you are seeking to inculcate?

3. How can you increase the leadership level of those under your leadership?

Chapter 16
By Many Prayers and Tears – Spiritual Leadership in The Salvation Army
by General Eva Burrows (Retired)

BOOKS on Christian leadership are continually being published and most begin by telling the reader that the greatest need of the church today is for leaders. Mind you, it is much the same in the secular world. Leadership is a word on everyone's lips. Articles in magazines, discussions on TV and radio, and books, books, books… There seems to be general agreement that there is much less leadership around than there used to be, and there's much less around than there should be!

An American military general recently said in his retirement speech, 'The trouble with the American army is that there are too many managers and not enough leaders.'

In his book entitled *Where Have All the Leaders Gone?*, Lee Iacocca stated 'The trouble with many organisations and churches is that they are over-managed and under-led.'[179] This discussion concerning the difference between a leader and a manager is a constant theme these days, and highlights the need not just for an organiser and administrator at the head of a company or a church, but for a visionary who leads the way ahead. In Christian circles this is being termed 'transformational leadership' – what Leighton Ford [President of Leighton Ford Ministries] called 'leading edge leadership', the type of leadership that empowers positive change and motivates followers to do more than they ever thought possible, leadership that causes people to say, 'I want to follow him.'

What is the difference between spiritual leadership, and any other kind of leadership? In many ways secular and spiritual leaders draw on many common insights and skills, but spiritual leaders have a big plus both in what they seek to achieve and how they go about achieving it. What spiritual leadership is seeking to achieve is the glory of God, so Church and Army leadership is not about impressive theological credentials so much as the sheer need for the leaders to care about the Body of Christ, to watch over its people and lead them forward as learners of Christ. That is why leaders take Jesus as the definitive model of spiritual leadership.

In setting down my thoughts on spiritual leadership, I do not wish to give a counsel of perfection, for no one has all the gifts, and there is no one set style or pattern of leadership. Researchers have never been able to satisfactorily define what makes one person rather than another a great leader. When Principal of the ICO, I held a Leadership Training Course for officers from the developing territories. At one session four highly esteemed retired Salvation Army leaders submitted themselves to a barrage of questions from the leader students. It was an electrifying couple of hours as there was revealed the forthright, military style of General Kitching, the scholarly, perceptive style of General Coutts, the decisive, almost surgical style of the famous missionary doctor Commissioner Williams, and the inspirational, motivational style of Commissioner Dalziel.

Whilst there are different styles according to personality traits, temperament, educational background, natural and spiritual gifts, there are common elements that make a Salvation Army spiritual leader effective in empowering his people. I share my thoughts on this matter with you.

Character

Spiritual leadership is not so much about something one does, but something one is. Of the various qualities of character needed, I would highlight:

Godliness

Allowing the Holy Spirit free operation in your life gives spiritual authority, which is far more powerful than intellectual ability or a dynamic personality. You stand before the people as God's representatives, his ambassadors, speaking for him.

Integrity

True genuineness. This means transparency, openness, no pretence. There is no credibility gap between what you say and how you behave.

Convictions

Holding firmly to what you believe, to your convictions about the Christian faith and The Salvation Army's principles and practice. You cannot teach to others what you are not sure about yourself. In his autobiography Nelson Mandela wrote: 'The key to survival is to have strong convictions.'

Servanthood

The role of a servant is the hallmark of a spiritual leader. The Spiritual Life Commission recommended that Salvation Army leadership at every level should conform to the biblical model of servant leadership. It clearly infers that spiritual leadership and servant leadership are one and the same.

Jesus himself defined leadership as service. When on the way to Jerusalem, in conversation with the self-seeking sons of Zebedee, he said that the one who would be powerful in his Kingdom must be servant of all. Then he went on to expand his teaching for the whole group of learners by using himself as an example: 'Even the Son of Man did not come to be served, but to serve, and to give his life as a ransom for many' (Mark 10:45).

A most powerful demonstration of servanthood was in the upper room on the night before his sacrificial death on Calvary, when Jesus washed the dirty feet of his learners with the hands of God. 'You call me "Teacher" and "Lord", and rightly so, for that is what I am. Now that I, your Lord and Teacher, have washed your feet, you also should wash one another's feet. I have set you an example that you should do as I have done for you' (John 13:13-15).

Jesus calls all spiritual leaders to that kind of servant-love, where no task is too humble, and no person so low that they cannot stoop to serve. He makes clear that it will involve suffering, but to suffer for Christ is a privilege, not a penalty.

I read of the principal of a theological college who told the students about to be ordained that they would find in their room his farewell gift. To their surprise, each received an envelope and inside was a piece of towelling inscribed, 'Keep this to remember you go out as servants, for Jesus' sake.'

Being a servant goes against the human grain. We don't even like the word, and avoid using it in the secular world. We invent euphemisms to enhance the names of some menial jobs.

Power is generally equated with position and status, but Jesus turned that power scale on its head by equating power with love. Because of his love, he had power with people, rather than power over people. The truest expression of love for Christ as spiritual leaders is to be his servant, and the servant of his people.

Being a servant leader doesn't mean you abdicate responsibility. Jesus the servant nevertheless knew that 'the Father had put all things under his power' (John 13:3). He had a strong sense of his calling and destiny, but he used it to serve rather than to 'lord it over others'. God approved and honoured his servanthood, for in the first Servant Song of the prophet Isaiah, God speaks; 'Here is my servant, whom I uphold, my chosen one in whom I delight' (Isaiah 42:1). Truly God still delights in the servant leaders of his Kingdom.

A spiritual leader is a visionary

The esteemed Anglican cleric John Stott [1921-2011] explained vision as 'a dissatisfaction with what is, and an insight into what could be. It begins with a disquiet about the status quo and a growing quest for an alternative.' Indeed leadership begins when a vision emerges, and a man or woman passionately seeks to bring that vision to reality. That person is no longer willing to leave things as they are, and seeks to lead others forward to face change and renewal.

Jesus was a man of vision. He had a vision of the Kingdom of God established on earth, where good would triumph over evil, where men and women would be delivered from their sins and made anew, when a new humanity would come into being and a new order be established of justice, freedom and equality for all. He was indignant about the conditions of his day. He was incensed by the bigotry of religious leaders. He was revolutionary in his thinking, and fearless in the pursuit of his dream.

In that vision Jesus lived, worked, taught, preached and healed. For that vision he gave his life to accomplish our redemption, and then commissioned his followers to go into the whole world and make all nations his learners.

Spiritual leaders of the Bible and Church history who made the greatest impression on their own generation were those who had vision to a high degree. Such was William Booth, who was dissatisfied with conditions as they were in Britain and in the Church, and with courage and holy optimism went out in faith to do 'the new thing' God wanted from him.

Visionary leaders are not afraid to fail, they set the pace, they dare to make bold and creative plans; they eschew the 'safety first' style; they adventure with God into new fields of ideas and service. They are focused on mission, not maintenance. However, it is not enough to have a vision. Men and women of vision need to be men and women of action and hard work. Without hard work, the vision vanishes, the dream evaporates; without a vision, the work loses direction, passion and fire.

A vision I had from God during my time as General was that The Salvation Army would return to Russia and other countries behind the Iron Curtain. The Lord gave me indicators, well in advance. Even before the Berlin Wall was demolished in 1989 a group of Russian Christians unexpectedly sang the Founder's song to me at an international Lausanne conference. Then the Lord thrust, almost before my nose, the words in Latin which I took as my motto: *carpe diem* – seize the day. Then he told me to get on with the job. Graciously he kept affirming that I was on the right track by sending money and personnel for the tasks. If the vision is of the Lord, work hard and he will bring it to fruition.

So vision is backed by courage, strengthened by faith and followed by decisive action. The leader then makes up their mind with the help of the Holy Spirit, and keeps to that decision, as the Lord prospers the plans.

A strong prayer life leads to spiritual authority and inspirational leadership

The power behind a strong spiritual leader is their relationship with God, and this is maintained and developed through prayer. If there is one area in which a spiritual leader should be ahead of their followers, it is in personal prayer life.

Daniel is a powerful example of such a leader whose prayer life was characterised by a holy awareness of God, discipline and intercession. To him God was supreme over all the earth, full of wisdom and might. So he habitually set aside times for prayer, no matter what the circumstances or what the pressure, to plead for God's mercy, grace and forgiveness. Today's spiritual leaders are often, metaphorically speaking, in the lion's den, but prayer will shut the lions' mouths.

Spiritual leadership is not automatically retained for, as Samson discovered, carelessness concerning the source and secret of his spiritual power brought failure, disgrace and destruction. 'He did not know that the Lord had departed from him' (Judges 16:20 *NASB*). We need to remember also that God deals most sternly with the shortcomings and sins of leaders, as Moses discovered when he was not permitted to enter the Promised Land.

There can be no substitute for prayer, not even ardent devotion to God's work, or a holy enthusiasm for mission. Bill Hybels, that frenetically active, world-famous Christian ministry leader, appropriately named one of his books, *Too Busy Not To Pray*.[180]

Henri Nouwen, in *The Way of the Heart: Desert Spirituality and Contemporary Ministry*,[181] writes that in prayer and solitude we get rid of 'the scaffolding of our lives', those artificial supports that prop us up and give us an unreal sense of our own importance and ability. In prayer, that scaffolding goes, and we know our dependence is on God.

The pastoral role as shepherd of the flock of God

Spiritual leaders have a genuine concern and love for the people they lead. This is their pastoral role as shepherds of the flock of God, which Jesus exemplified as the Good Shepherd, and explained in his teaching. Shepherd is a biblical term for a leader who empowers others, helping them grow, trusting them with responsibility, testing their commitment. He invests his life in his people, and produces leaders like himself.

A spiritual leader respects the people he leads. He works with the people available, never despising them, however weak they may be. He never blames them for his own failures; never reproves them for his own lack of achievement.

Jesus' learners were not an impressive bunch, but Jesus never disdained them. He grieved over them, was disappointed in them, was deserted by them, but he never disparaged them. Of God's ideal servant it is said, 'He won't brush aside the bruised and the hurt and he won't disregard the small and insignificant' (Isaiah 42:3 *The Message*).

Neither is a leader afraid of those he leads. Moses showed such generosity of spirit toward Eldad and Medad (Numbers 11:28-29), even when Joshua wanted them stopped from prophesying in apparent competition with Moses. It was a beautiful lesson.

A spiritual leader does not force out strong people under him/her, and replace them with more malleable people who are easily influenced. These are the people we call 'yes men', whose praise and admiration can never be sound advice. The biblical examples of 'yes men' were the false prophets. The true prophet Nathan, with his personal criticism of King David's adultery, was David's most valuable adviser

An effective spiritual leader helps to build a team spirit. Shepherd leadership is relational, not an authoritarian command requiring blind obedience. The shepherd cares for his people and wants to work alongside them. The term used in The Salvation Army nowadays is consultative leadership, working together, seeking consensus through the Holy Spirit, with no competitive spirit, no 'pulling rank'.

A strong sense of accountability

Accountability is an important word in use these days, in such fields as business and politics. A modern word, it is not seen in most Bible translations, where it is expressed as 'faithful stewardship', 'trustworthiness' or 'honesty in all dealings'.

Accountability is an important quality for all Christian leaders. Jesus spoke a lot about it especially in such parables as those of the talents, the sheep and the goats, and the rich farmer.

A leader's first accountability is to God, for the gifts he has been given and the opportunities of leadership. I remember telling General Arnold Brown once that he was 'a 10-talent officer'. He said, 'That's terrifying. Just think how inadequate my answers will be when I stand before Christ.' The words of Jesus were well understood by him: 'From everyone who has been given much, much will be demanded; and from the one who has been entrusted with much, much more will be asked' (Luke 12:48).

A leader's accountability is also to The Salvation Army which has given him training, a place of service and the privilege of leadership. The Salvation Army has a right to call us to account for the way we are using the opportunities and privileges we have.

I remember seeing a notebook of William Booth in which he would write down donations handed to him after speaking at meetings. Two consecutive entries were: 'From Mr Cory, 200 pounds' [a very large sum in those days], followed by: 'From a poor woman, one shilling'.

A spiritual leader is also accountable to themself; how they use this one life they have; making the best use of time and talents; watching their motivation; learning to know themself. In Acts 20:28, Paul reminds the leaders of the church at Ephesus to 'Keep watch over yourselves', before advising them to keep watch over their people.

Spiritual leaders know their own worth, their own strengths and weaknesses. This gives an inner security that enables them to free others to become their best, enabling them to discover, develop, dedicate and deploy their gifts for the Kingdom. In one of his books, General John Larsson relates a Jewish parable which states that when we go to stand before the judgement seat of God, he will not ask, 'Why weren't you a Moses?' He will ask, 'Why weren't you yourself?'

Availability and self-discipline

Good stewards are always available to their master and to their people. Availability to God is a spiritual leader's first duty, a total surrender of the self to God's control, seeking his will, finding out his instructions and designing plans to his direction. This spiritual availability is essential to the success of mission planning. I recall reading the phrase 'a covenant of availability', and I commend it. It is Kingdom-availability, as a leader devotes their gifts, their whole life to defend and grow the Kingdom of Christ.

Availability to their people makes heavy demands on leaders, on their physical, intellectual and emotional energies, and on their time. That is why spiritual leaders need to have a disciplined lifestyle, involving time management, establishing priorities, without being tyrannised by the clock. It is here that Jesus is the role model, for his was the beautifully balanced life of involvement and detachment, action and contemplation, doing and being.

A Russian proverb states: 'What would you think of a wood chopper who was too busy chopping wood to take time out to sharpen his axe?'

Areas of vulnerability

Before concluding this paper, it would be wise to make reference to some particular areas of vulnerability for spiritual leaders which they should heed. Because they are human, leaders will still make mistakes and errors in judgement, often because they haven't taken the trouble to find out all the facts or they have taken a decision in too much haste without adequate thought or prayer. So there is no need to think that spiritual leadership guarantees infallibility. No matter what a person's responsibility, to freely admit a mistake is strong leadership. It is the weak leader who covers up in self-defence.

To quote General Frederick Coutts: 'Leaders can have few private weaknesses. Our weaknesses have a way of getting known by others.

We may think they are private, but some keen observer among those being led will notice them. We can't complain about that. We occupy public positions by God's will. We must accept the hazards of our responsibility.'

It often happens that when a person rises in position, even in the Church, the tendency to pride increases. If not checked, that attitude will disqualify the person in God's eyes for further responsibility in his service. 'The Lord detests all the proud of heart' (Proverbs 16:5).

When I was the TC in Scotland, some Salvationists often used a phrase in prayer, 'Hide the commissioner behind the Cross.' I reflected on it often. If one is hidden behind the Cross, one will view the world and the mission through the Cross, and that is a great antidote to pride.

History teaches us that personality cults can develop even around spiritual leaders, and followers become awestruck by the leader's celebrity status. Paul faced this problem in the church at Corinth where some favoured Apollos and others Paul. In exasperation Paul writes, 'What, after all, is Apollos? And what is Paul? Only servants, through whom you came to believe – as the Lord has assigned to each his task' (1 Corinthians 3:5).

There is no fault in being pleased and encouraged when one's service is appreciated, but one needs to keep in mind Jesus' words, 'Woe to you when all men speak well of you' (Luke 6:26 *NIV 1984*).

The great preacher Spurgeon said: 'Success can go to my head, and will, unless I remember that it is God who accomplishes the work, and he can continue to do so without my help, and with other means.'

The spiritual leader is human and subject to nature's laws, just as anyone else. If he breaks physical laws, he pays a physical price. In my case, at a time of demanding leadership, I suffered a heart attack at the age of 50. In a letter of good wishes, a retired leader nevertheless admonished me, 'Remember you can't ask God Almighty to bless a seven-day week. It is against his holy ordinance.'

Spiritual leaders need to beware of pushing themselves to exhaustion, or 'burn out' – the mental anguish of making difficult and unpopular decisions, the strain of loneliness when the making of those decisions cannot be shared – such are heavy burdens on our psyche. This is when the balanced lifestyle is an essential; a style Commissioner Caughey Gauntlett used to call 'relaxed intensity'.

Finally, I need to refer to personal ambition, which can diminish a leader's spiritual effectiveness. Ambition in itself is not wrong. It is the motivation behind the ambition that makes it a holy ambition or a worldly ambition. The Bible teaches that any ambition which centres around oneself is unworthy, but an ambition that has the glory of God as its centre is not only legitimate but praiseworthy. So spiritual leaders must carefully watch their personal motives. As Jeremiah states, 'Should you then seek great things for yourself? Do not seek them' (Jeremiah 45:5).

The Salvation Army structure, its ranks, its seeming ladder of command, can cause a leader to seek position for his own prestige, power and reputation. That is one of the subtle temptations for those who lead. Even the sacred occasion of the Last Supper was marred by the selfish strife among the disciples.

The ambition of which God approves is pure, noble, touched by self-sacrifice and self-denial. Perhaps the best way to conclude this paper is to quote from Commissioner Samuel Brengle. He was a man of scholarship as well as great spiritual power. He outlined the road to spiritual authority and leadership in these challenging words: '...[it] is not won...by promotion, but by many prayers, tears and confessions of sin...It is not gained by seeking great things for ourselves, but rather, like Paul, by counting those things that were gain loss for Christ...That is a great price, but it must be unflinchingly paid by him who would be not merely a nominal, but a real spiritual leader of men...whose power is recognized... and felt in Heaven, earth and Hell.'[182]

Reading Guide

If you tally up all these characteristics of a great leader it can get pretty intimidating. We have discussed servant leadership earlier in the book. Visionary leadership is an enormous blessing to the body of believers. And true spiritual vision comes through revelation from God via time invested with him. General Burrows connects these keys with strong prayer that is accompanied by spiritual authority and provides inspirational leadership.

A Field for Exploits

She emphasises that true spiritual leaders are shepherds of the flock of God. Accountability and self discipline are essential components of leadership. General Burrows also highlights areas of vulnerability: error in judgement, pride and ambition.

Discussion Starters

1. We agree that accountability is important. How can we put protections in place against the errors of vulnerability? How can we train our learners to do it in their future leadership?

2. Authority and power seem based in prayer. How can we emphasise this in our leader training?

3. Vision is critical to the salvation war. How can we stimulate vision and visioning in our leader training?

---

[179] Lee Iacocca, *Where Have All The Leaders Gone?*, Scribner (Simon & Schuster), New York, 2008.

[180] Bill Hybels, *Too Busy Not To Pray*, Inter-Varsity Press, Nottingham, 2011.

[181] Henri Nouwen, *The Way of the Heart: Desert Spirituality and Contemporary Ministry*, Seabury Press, Minneapolis, MN, 1981.

[182] Samuel Logan Brengle, *The Soul-Winner's Secret*, 36-37, The Salvation Army, New York, NY 1903.

Chapter 17
21st Century Leadership
by General Eva Burrows (Retired)

What kind of officers/leaders do we anticipate producing?
IN AN issue of the magazine *Christianity Today*, I saw an advertisement for a theological college called 'The Kings Seminary'. It stated its purpose in this challenging statement:

Our aim is to prepare leaders for the church of the 21st century who are:
- *Ministry-minded.*
- *Culturally sensitive.*
- *Theologically balanced.*
- *Evangelistically passionate.*
- *Holy Spirit-empowered.*

That's some statement to describe leaders of this millennium! But those qualities are what I hope will describe our learners as they come to leadership, for they are essential for those who will be effective and adaptable to change as leaders in God's Army and the Church of the future.

So I would like to look in depth at each of these qualities as a challenge to us today. I am sharing this from my own personal experience – not from some popular book on Christian leadership – though there are scores of them being published these days. And mostly they call for leadership of a new quality; leadership that inspires, that makes things happen, that sets the vision, communicates the mission, manages constructive change, makes a passionate call to follow – and has the thrill, the joy, of seeing many respond and follow: transformational leadership.

Ministry-minded

Leaders must constantly be concerned to discover the means of ministry that will make the Army effective. There are many styles of ministry the learners will study, but to me there is one supreme style – the ideal method of ministry – and that is incarnational ministry in the style of Jesus Christ.

Jesus said to his learners: 'As the Father has sent me, I am sending you' (John 20:21). That's us as leaders! We are to serve in the same spirit as he did with his mission statement 'to seek and save the lost'. Jesus, by his incarnation, by an incredibly humbling process, laid aside the privileges of the Godhead, was born as a human being to share our life. He is our exemplar.

Jesus need not have been born to poverty in a lowly manger. He need not have worked as a common labourer. He need not have endured ridicule and persecution. But he did. He identified with us human beings. For our sakes, he faced whatever it cost to show God's love and win men and women to his kingdom. No wonder his message was powerful. The service of Christ will involve leaders in incarnational ministry, identifying with those they seek to evangelise.

Following the dreadful race riots and violence of 1981 in Brixton, an impoverished black ghetto in London, a commission was set up to investigate the situation. Lord Scarman was the chairman. When he was giving an address to Salvationist youth leaders, one asked the question, 'What is the solution?'

Lord Scarman replied, 'That's simple. Go and live there.' That is incarnational ministry. It costs something to do that. To go and live there. To share the life of those we seek to win for Christ. To step out of the comfort zone of so much of Christianity today, and step into the danger zone of daring, risky incarnational living. Are we equipping leaders to be prepared to live within these situations? To identify? To empathise?

Can you drink of the cup that Jesus drank (see Mark 10:38)? It costs a lot to identify with another person, to get into his skin, learn his language; whether it is the tongue of the Dayaks of Kalimantan [Borneo], or whether it is a matter of shedding our familiar theological terms for the language of pop culture or the motorcycle gang.

Max Warren, in his book *I Believe in the Great Commission*,[183] declares: 'No Christian has a right to feel comfortable as long as there are any, anywhere, who do not know Christ.' Are our learners prepared to think about how much it will cost them to serve Christ? Are they being prepared to spend and be spent for Christ?

A caring ministry is powerful too, when we demonstrate that Christ is alive by sharing the hurts, heartaches and needs of those about us. John said it well: 'Dear children, let us not love with words or tongue but with actions and in truth' (1 John 3:18 *NIV 1984*). And C.S. Lewis said it graphically in *The Screwtape Letters*:[184] 'Wormwood, it is not necessary to make people wicked. Just make them indifferent. Don't worry about getting people to do bad things, just let them do nothing at all. Provide me with people who do not care.'

Jesus was so different from that. He showed the meaning of caring involvement. He was concerned with the whole person. He healed the broken victims of society. He cared for people with tortured minds. He opened the eyes of the blind – the physically blind and the spiritually blind. He fed the hungry. He announced good news to the poor – the economically poor and the spiritually poor. He was the greatest teacher the world has ever seen, but he wasn't a word merchant. He had a practical ministry. And that is why he was so powerful. He lived it out in action. We must equip learners for that kind of ministry. That is why, again and again in the Gospel stories, Jesus condemns the person who refuses to get involved.

That is why he told the story of the good Samaritan. I once heard an African pastor preach on the parable of the good Samaritan. He said, 'There are three kinds of people in this story. There are the robbers; they do bad. Then there are the Samaritans; they do good. Then there are the religious men; they're the people who do nothing.' That's a fresh interpretation. Jesus told the story to show that we should get involved, like the Samaritan traveller. To do whatever it costs to meet human need of every kind with Christlike compassion.

Ministry of social action and social justice

Leaders of the 21st century will need to be increasingly concerned for the poor and dispossessed, those neglected by governments who have become obsessed with economic rationalism; the uncaring face of political policies. The Church, including the Army, will have to take upon itself the burden of the underprivileged and poor, working within the social context of the local church. For the Army, it must be a rediscovery of our bias for the poor. Are our learners being equipped for that?

It is a charge to us from Christ, which we cannot ignore. That is not some so-called social gospel; that is the true gospel. And that is a thrilling and demanding challenge to the leaders of the Army and the leaders of the Church of this millennium.

Culturally sensitive

We are living in a world which is becoming increasingly culturally diverse. Leaders of the future need to become more culturally sensitive, able to understand the need to contextualise the message of truth. Salvationists previously thought of contextualisation in terms of communicating the gospel worldwide, in other lands, often called missionary lands. But the matter is on our own doorstep.

We in the Western churches now freely admit to the mistakes of the past in transmitting the gospel cross-culturally. Missionaries so often disregarded culture, and were suspicious of it, while ignorant of the fact that they were transmitting a gospel already overloaded with the baggage from their own Western culture. Such evangelical imperialism is no longer acceptable. Our attitudes and understanding have changed; we do a lot better now.

Let us never forget the example of the early Church. At Antioch, Christianity changed from a Jewish sect to a religion of the world. In the church at Antioch there were Africans, Cypriots and Greeks: a multi-cultural ministry. Did you realise that black hands were among those laid on the heads of Paul and Barnabas when they were set forth to evangelise in Asia Minor and Europe? (Acts 13:1-3).

The apostle Paul worked effectively in many cultures. While refusing to change his message to please men, he would go to any lengths to avoid giving offence or putting needless difficulties in the way of people's understanding and response to the gospel. 'Though I am free and belong to no one, I have made myself a slave to everyone, to win as many as possible. To the Jews I became like a Jew, to win the Jews. To those under the law I became like one under the law (though I myself am not under the law), so as to win those under the law. To those not having the law I became like one not having the law (though I am not free from God's law but am under Christ's law), so as to win those not having the law. To the weak I became weak, to win the weak. I have become all things to all people so that by all possible means I might save some' (1 Corinthians 9:19-22).

Paul didn't throw truth at people. He went out of his way to get alongside them, to start thinking from where they were, whether in Greece or Rome. He avoided anything that would prejudice them against the gospel. He sought to be relevant to the context of his hearers.

Thank God we have come back to that approach. Today there is a new awareness of, and respect for, cultural differences. A new desire to make the gospel culturally relevant and authentic, while being faithful to the revealed truth in Jesus Christ. That is what we mean by contextualisation, and all leaders must grasp its importance for the growth of the Army.

I see it as a key to the ministry of the Church today, not only with people of other cultures such as Portuguese, Laotians, Koreans, Vietnamese, Chinese, but the sub-cultures of Australia, the pop culture of modern youth, the baby boomers and generation X, the postmoderns, the New Agers, who each have a language and set of values of their own.

All leaders should be sensitive to this and develop cross-cultural ministries, helping their people to come to a mature, relevant and contemporary experience of the faith, and claim it as their own. This will also require various styles of programmes and strategies, from house groups to the church in the cinema or shopping mall; contextualising music, worship styles and atmosphere, and the language of effective communication.

Theologically balanced

Leaders in this millennium will need to have a sound grasp of the main theological and ethical issues that present such challenges in society and the Church in today's pluralism. They will need to work through these issues and develop strong convictions which they can articulate with confidence and spiritual authority. Such issues as genetic engineering, abortion, euthanasia, pornography, gambling, environmental issues, racism. They will need not just to know the Army's position but also to have a strong personal understanding of these issues, many of which have the potential to fragment the Church. There are no simplistic, easy, pat answers. Leaders must have intelligently thought through these matters, for it is the Church which must give the moral lead.

Then there are the theological issues such as the reliability of the Scriptures, the uniqueness of Christ as Lord and only Saviour, the centrality of the Resurrection in the Christian faith, the reality of sin and redemption, and so on.

Evangelistically passionate

Leaders in the 21st century will need to be powerfully focused on the great commission, passionately seeking to make learners for Christ, winning for Christ those who have never believed before, and those who have turned away through disillusionment and disenchantment. This will exercise them in creative methods of evangelism, and in adaptation of the means of communicating the gospel. This is a challenge when seeking to reach the postmodern generations with the truths of the gospel.

Brian Walsh in his fine paper 'Postmodernity and the Church: Ten Things You Need to Know',[185] reminds us that an over-intellectualisation of the faith will have little effect on people who have come to know that rational argument can be twisted to mean whatever the speaker wants it to mean. He writes: 'What we have always needed, and need more in this generation, is the Word made flesh.' That's why we communicate the gospel best by lifting up Jesus.

We do not lift up:

- A system of theology and religion, because people need more than theology and religion when the storms of life bring tragedy and heartache.
- A moral code, because people are not motivated by a set of ethical rules.
- A programme for social action, because social reform, while helpful, will not transform a man or woman's character.

No, we must lift up Christ. The gospel *is* Jesus Christ. He alone can give us life, offer us forgiveness, share our sufferings, meet our needs. Every learner needs to grasp this as a non-negotiable.

The Early Church is our example. The central theme of the whole tapestry of the Early Church's proclamation was Jesus Christ, crucified and risen again. Whether in Jerusalem where, 'Day after day, in the temple courts and from house to house, they never stopped teaching and proclaiming the good news that Jesus is the Messiah' (Acts 5:42) or in Samaria, where Philip 'began preaching Christ to them', or as Paul, moving in Europe, would say, 'I determined to know nothing among you except Jesus Christ' (1 Corinthians 2:2 *NASB*).

Wesley's powerful secret was: 'I came to this town and I offered them Christ.' Jesus is the attraction. So while the brilliant theologians may be closeted in their college towers trying to set out the essentials of the gospel message, I remind them of the essential: to lift up Jesus Christ as Saviour and Lord of all. This must be the conviction of every learner, every leader – understood, experienced and put into practice.

Holy Spirit-empowered

More than ever before, leaders must be Holy Spirit-empowered people. We are in an age when the doctrine of the Holy Spirit has come out of the mystic shadows into the glorious light of experience. The Holy Spirit need no longer be an enigma, a mystery, for we now see him to be God at work in the world, and God at work in you and me.

He is indispensable in our life as Christians and in the growth of the Church. And as Christian leaders we need to be Spirit-filled, Spirit-directed and Spirit-empowered. What's the good of admitting the existence of the Holy Spirit if we have no experience of him? He provides the power for ordinary believers like you and me to live, serve and lead in ways that would otherwise be impossible. He is God's agent for change in our personal lives and in the Church. He is essential to our life-changing experience of salvation as he convicts of sin and leads us to faith in Christ. Then that change continues through the Spirit's sanctifying power as we are being conformed to the image of Christ. He changes us in character and motivation as he develops in us the fruit of the Spirit.

He is God's agent for unity and growth in the Church

After all, the Holy Spirit brought the Church into being: 'For by one Spirit are we all baptised into one body' (1 Corinthians 12:13 *KJV*), the members serving one another in love. A bond of unity, worship and service. He does that still through the gifts of the Spirit which equip people to empowering ministry. Spirit-filled leaders build Spirit-filled churches and Spirit-filled churches are growing churches. We can use all the techniques of church growth principles, we can strategise with skill, take Willow Creek ideas, but unless that work is Spirit-directed, it will only be a box of tricks.

He is indispensable as our teacher, tutor and educator

We have Jesus' promise for that: 'But when he, the Spirit of truth, comes, he will guide you into all the truth. He will not speak on his own; he will speak only what he hears, and he will tell you what is yet to come' (John 16:13).

Note the reference to *all* the truth. The Holy Spirit doesn't focus just on some things Jesus taught, and leave out other things that don't please us. That would be a lopsided Christianity. He is not interested in partial Christian experience. He will guide us into *everything* Jesus taught. That's why we need Holy Spirit-empowered leaders. When leaders are Spirit-filled, they will be counselled by the Holy Spirit. He will give wise, challenging, trustworthy counselling. We remember that's what Jesus said when he promised, 'I'm sending you *another* counsellor.' The Holy Spirit is indispensable in the life of every leader in the Church of the 21st century. May we train learners to be leaders who are ministry-minded, culturally-sensitive, theologically-balanced, evangelistically-passionate and Holy Spirit-empowered.

Reading Guide

General Burrows provides keys to 21st century spiritual leadership:
- Ministry-minded.
- Culturally-sensitive.
- Theologically-balanced.
- Evangelistically-passionate.
- Holy Spirit-empowered.

It is quite a collection of attributes. The challenge is to be intentional in our training to ensure that our learners are trained to teach and embrace for themselves these components of effective 21st century spiritual leadership. We need to cultivate an environment in which our learners grasp this outside of a formal curriculum. This can be benefitted by conversation (regularly talking up these aspects), modelling (living and engaging in these things in a manner that is attractive and brings credibility), and encouragement (stimulating love and good deeds).

Discussion Starters

1. How do we emphasise these components in our leader training? How can we maintain credibility in our leadership in these areas?

2. How can we enrich the influence of the environment we are nurturing in which our learners are to experience ministry-mindedness, cultural sensitivity, theological balance, evangelistic passion, and Holy Spirit empowerment?

---

[183] Max Warren, *I Believe in the Great Commission*, Hodder & Stoughton, USA, 1976.
[184] C.S. Lewis, *The Screwtape Letters*, 60th anniversary edition, HarperCollins, London, 2002.
[185] Brian Walsh, 'Postmodernity and the Church: Ten Things You Need to Know', *Good Idea*, 3.4 (Winter), Institute of Evangelism, Wycliffe College, USA, 1996.

Chapter 18
Conclusion – 'Ten to Take Away'
by Major Stephen Court

SO, there you have it: a potted version of the combined wisdom of Salvation Army leadership throughout the movement's history on training leaders. We have heard from several Generals and some other outstanding Salvationist thinkers and practitioners from around the world and throughout our history. Representative teaching from each of the four International Training Councils – 1925, 1951, 1974 and 2001 – has enriched our understanding of this important subject. And, remember, these people are writing with proven experience. These teachings actually work. These principles, taught through our history, established a sacrificial, ultra-revivalist movement that sped around the world, transforming great swathes of the world's most fragile and vulnerable regions with leaders trained up from the people groups they were destined to serve.

The spiritual consequences of our mission effectiveness are marked in sociological terms as 'redemption and lift'. Converts from indigence and addiction get settled and clean up their lives, hold down jobs, restore relationships and provide a Christian upbringing for their children, who finish school and qualify for better jobs and can afford nicer homes, and so on. This means, among other things, that as some of us experience the social benefits of righteous living, we must continue reminding ourselves of the fundamentals of Salvation Army leader training.

Here are 'Ten to Take Away':

1. We convey a peculiar message – Saved to Save. And we are fully saved to fully save.

2. We infuse our training with Salvationism. This is not just another seminary or discipleship school.

3. We create for our learners a field for exploits in which they

can experiment and risk and innovate and initiate for the glory of God.

4. We believe that change is possible, and necessary, in character. Hallelujah!

5. We aim much deeper than just the transmission of knowledge and skills. We aim at inner transformation by the Holy Spirit's power.

6. We raise up evangelists who evangelise effectively and who train and lead their people to evangelise effectively, remembering that we love to fight and we fight with love.

7. We recognise that a myriad of dynamics affect how we train, and we are flexible and sensitive to culture and context as well as adaptable in terms of justice, mercy and service, while maintaining the essential principles of salvation.

8. We dream and plan and prepare for the changing conditions of the salvation war in coming years with visionary leadership.

9. We have thought through the complexities of Salvation Army leadership biblically, spiritually and practically, and are positioned to multiply leaders who understand who, how, what and why we are as we are.

10. We are committed to effectively transforming learners into leaders in the great salvation war to win the world for Jesus.

May God quicken, inspire and empower you in your own leadership and in your leadership training in raising up leaders who perform great exploits for our great God and Saviour Jesus Christ, to the end of seeing all people come into a saving relationship with Jesus.

Discussion Starters

1. What did you learn that you did not know?
2. How can these lessons change your own leadership?
3. How can this affect your leader training?
4. What process can you follow to adapt and implement the lessons on your front?

Potted Biographies of Authors

General Bramwell Booth
Eldest son of William Booth and second international leader of The Salvation Army. He was the architect of the Army's administration as the movement expanded around the world. He helped shape Army culture through holiness teaching, writing and youth councils.

Mrs General Florence Booth
A gifted leader, organiser and forthright preacher. Before marriage to Bramwell, she was a pioneer officer in Europe. She later became British Commissioner during her husband's Generalship and wrote powerfully-worded books on Salvationism and officership.

Commissioner Catherine Bramwell-Booth
A decade on the training staff preceded her oversight of Army work in Europe. She was a long-time commissioner and an authoritative writer. Her masterful biography of her grandmother, Catherine Booth, led to fame when aged in her 90s through a series of appearances on television chat shows in the UK.

General Albert Orsborn
Great preacher, orator and poet, General Orsborn oversaw post-Second World War consolidation of the Army, and blessed the movement with many powerful songs, especially about the Cross. He oversaw the influential International Youth Congress of 1950 and wrote an important autobiography, *The House of My Pilgrimage*, giving personal insights into early Salvation Army history.

General Erik Wickberg

Statesmanlike and an outstanding theologian, General Wickberg was a wise administrator. After influential leadership throughout Europe, he brought an academic sensibility to the world leadership, carefully guiding the Army through an era of significant change.

General Arnold Brown

Particularly gifted in bringing the Army's message and mission to the public at large, General Brown was also a powerful preacher and soul winner. He pioneered the Army's mass communication in radio and television, revolutionised public relations and updated the Army's administrative system.

General Eva Burrows

Often called 'the people's General', General Burrows brought two decades of African and Asian experience to bear on international leadership. She restructured IHQ administration, created the United Kingdom with the Republic of Ireland Territory, and piloted The Salvation Army's return to formerly communist eastern Europe.

General Paul A. Rader

A keen missiologist, General Rader served for 22 years in Korea, followed by leadership in the USA. He left a legacy of aggressive strategy worldwide, elucidating his vision in powerful messages as well as setting ambitious international goals for conversions and new corps and soldiers.

Commissioner Clive Adams

Served in appointments in his home territory of South Africa, becoming Training Principal. He came on to the international scene when organising the International Youth Forum in South Africa in 1996. Commissioner Adams is currently TC in the Norway, Iceland and the Færoes Territory.

Dr Jonathan Raymond

President of Trinity Western University in Canada, Dr Raymond has served in leadership positions in three Christian colleges, is a widely published author and is co-editor of the Salvationist journal *Word & Deed*. He has been a member of the International Doctrine Council.

Major Stephen Court

Major Court has pioneered new corps, congregations and outposts in his homeland of Canada and in Australia. He was also training principal in the Australia Southern Territory. While his thinking is deeply embedded in Army history and mission, he is a creative thinker and innovator. He has written several books.

A Pilgrim's Song
the autobiography of Jarl Wahlström

The English language edition of the autobiography of Jarl Wahlström – the twelfth General of The Salvation Army and the first Finnish officer to be elected to that role. In this book, first published in Finnish in 1989, the author describes how, as one of God's pilgrims, he was uniquely privileged to witness the work of The Salvation Army in some of the remotest parts of the world. Jarl Wahlström served as General from 1981 to 1986, and throughout these pages the reader will sense how he thanks God for his pilgrimage and the hope of an eternal goal.

192pp (paperback), 41 photographs
ISBN 978-0-85412-845-7

Called Up – Pages from the Story of my Life
the autobiography of Erik Wickberg

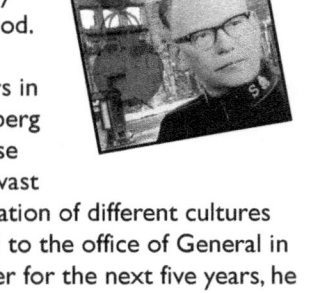

The English language edition of the autobiography of Erik Wickberg – the ninth General of The Salvation Army and a testimony to the rich life to be found in the service of God. This book, first published in Swedish in 1978, describes how, having spent his formative years in Sweden, Germany and Switzerland, Erik Wickberg then served as a Salvation Army officer in those countries as well as the United Kingdom. His vast knowledge of languages and thorough appreciation of different cultures stood him in good stead when he was elected to the office of General in 1969. Serving as the Army's international leader for the next five years, he oversaw and visited many aspects of the Army's ministry on every continent. This book provides a moving and colourful account of his life, including fascinating insights into his role as liaison officer in Sweden during the years of the Second World War.

168pp (paperback), 13 photographs
ISBN 978-0-85412-846-4

Can be purchased from any Salvation Army trade or supplies department and online at www.amazon.co.uk